THE OPEN-BORDERS NETWORK

THE OPEN-BORDERS NETWORK

How a Web of Ethnic Activists, Journalists,
Corporations, Politicians, Lawyers, and Clergy
Undermine U.S. Border Security and National Sovereignty

Kevin Lamb

REPRESENTATIVE GOVERNMENT PRESS

Lexington, Virginia

Copyright © 2009

American Research Foundation, Inc.
P.O. Box 20966
Raleigh, NC 27619

Published in the United States
by Representative Government Press

First edition 2007
Revised edition 2009

To: Courtney, Katie, and Mary

Breathes there the man with soul so dead
Who never to himself hath said
This is my own, my native land!

—**Sir Walter Scott**

CONTENTS

INTRODUCTION

❧

INCREASED PUBLIC VIGILANCE TO reform and enforce America's immigration laws prompted congressional action to rectify public concerns about the lack of border security and ineffective enforcement of existing immigration laws. Uncontrolled illegal immigration remains the focal point of widespread public indignation in recent years. *Time* and *Newsweek* magazines featured immigration in their cover stories of April 10, 2006, the former focusing on the larger question of immigration policy and the latter concentrating on more elusive aspects of citizenship and illegal immigration.[1] The public opinion poll published in *Time* showed that 68 percent of those surveyed considered illegal immigration as either "extremely serious" or "very serious" while only 8 percent considered the problem of illegal immigration as "not very serious." Eighty-two percent of those polled believed the U.S. was "not doing enough" along its borders to keep illegal immigrants out of the country. The *Time* poll is one of several surveys in recent years that highlight public concerns over illegal immigration. "A *Washington Post*-ABC News poll taken in mid-December [2005] found Americans alarmed by the federal government's failure to do more to block the flow of illegal immigration" into the U.S.[2]

Over a two-year span (2005-2007) members of the 109th and 110th Congress grappled with immigration reform legislation but ultimately failed to pass a "comprehensive" bill that

1

for many seemed to be one step forward and three back. The Comprehensive Immigration Reform Act of 2007 would have provided "funding for 300 miles of vehicle barriers, 105 camera and radar towers, and 20,000 more Border Patrol agents"[3] but also provided legal status and a path to full citizenship for millions of illegal aliens currently residing in the United States. Despite legislative attempts in the 109th and 110th Congress to change America's immigration laws, with pressure from the Bush Administration to pass these "comprehensive" reforms, the measures failed to become law.

This congressional deadlock — the inability of U.S. policymakers to overhaul America's immigration laws — underscores a major theme of this book: the greater national interest to fortify our borders and protect against invasions are being sacrificed to the special interests of minority ethnic groups. Lawmakers deadlocked on these immigration reforms, in part, because of their inability to reconcile their constituents' desire to clamp down on illegal immigration with highly aggressive, well-organized ethnic constituency groups.

During a question and answer period of a workshop presentation to immigration reform activists meeting in Kansas City, Missouri, in the spring of 2006, Steven Camarota, director of research at the Center for Immigration Studies, explained the difference that existed between organized advocates representing the mass-immigrant, open-borders constituency and grassroots citizen-activists promoting immigration restriction. Fulltime lobbyists representing the interests of the former, Camarota noted, would easily fill up a hotel conference room, while he could "count on one hand" the equivalent representatives working for immigration restriction.

To illustrate the point, that weekend's workshop presentation in the spring of 2006, sponsored by the Federation for American Immigration Reform (FAIR), attracted a few dozen local activists. On that same weekend, mass demonstrations clogged the streets of Los Angeles and other metropolitan areas with hundreds of thousands of open-border advocates. Demonstrators, largely driven by left-wing activists, successfully shut down businesses as thousands of Hispanic workers opted to protest or stay at home and not show up for work. The open-border demonstrations were organized to pressure the outcome of pending congressional legislation that would allow for another amnesty.

Despite public opinion polls that show overwhelming public concerns about the steady annual influx of illegal immigrants and the lack of border security and control by federal and state authorities, organized public interest groups — from civil libertarians to anarchists to radical socialist and communist organizations — took to the streets in an effort to advance a radical open-borders agenda. In a show of political muscle, these well-organized demonstrations showcased the collective unity and growing clout of Latinos to promote their ethnic minority agenda (the liberation of Aztlan) ahead of Middle America and the national interest.

This book attempts to provide some much-needed reflection on why there is such a lop-sided disparity of organized groups representing the interests of "open-borders," mass-immigration advocates and citizen-activist groups representing the interests of Middle America — patriotic citizens who seek tougher enforcement of our nation's borders and who prefer a stable reduction of immigration levels. Organized groups representing the interests and objectives of an open-borders agenda, promoting higher levels of mass immigration and cultivating the relaxation of laws enforcing our border security requirements (catching, detaining, and deporting illegal aliens) are working to not only undermine border security, U.S. immigration laws, and the overall national interest, but to revolutionize our cultural, political, and national traditions. Organized lobbies, as Jeffrey M. Berry noted in his influential study *The Interest Group Society*, are an intricate part of the U.S. political system in working to influence public policy. Under scrutiny in this brief analysis are the various public interest groups — largely on the political left — but also across the political spectrum (including organized labor and business interests) working to promote the global migration of Third World peoples, dismantle our national sovereignty, and transform the core culture of America's national character. The following chapters, intended as a brief overview on this vast subject, highlight the special interest groups championing a "borderless" society—from ethnic lobbies to the corporate, labor, legal, political, and religious elites—and why the national interest is subordinate to a borderless agenda. Like an anaconda, the grip of the open-borders network is pervasive and deadly, slowly squeezing the life out of our communities and culture.

Endnotes

1. *Time*, "Who Gets to be an American? Inside the immigration debate that is dividing the nation," April 10, 2006: 30-43. *Newsweek*, "Illegals Under Fire," Arian Campo-Flores, April 10, 2006: 28-39.
2. Dan Balz, "Political Splits on Immigration Reflect Voters' Ambivalence," *Washington Post*, January 3, 2006: A7.
3. http://en.wikipedia.org/wiki/Comprehensive_Immigration_Reform_Act_of_2007

FUNDING THE OPEN-BORDERS NETWORK
Immigrant Ethnic Lobbies & Philanthropic Foundations

ঙ৯ৡৎ

> In a less than perfect world, the allocation of rights
> based on territory must be defended if a ruinous
> breeding race is to be avoided. It is unlikely that
> civilization and dignity can survive everywhere;
> but better in a few places than in none. Fortunate
> minorities act as the trustees of a civilization that is
> threatened by uninformed good intentions.
>
> —Garrett Hardin[1]

WHEN IT COMES TO ADVANCING goals, objectives, and agendas, groups that are well-organized, and consequently well-funded, will eventually triumph over the unorganized, underrepresented, and underfunded. This is the overall truism that emerges from examining the organizational structure and effectiveness of successful interest groups. The same can be said of the organizations that comprise the open-borders network. No matter how actively engaged grassroots, patriotic Middle Americans are in trying to *individually* register their views by writing their congressman or publishing letters-to-the-editor in their local newspaper or simply casting a vote, in a pluralistic representative democracy such activities are no match for the well-organized open-borders network and ethnic-immigrant lobbies. Those who remain unorganized will eventually find themselves unmatched and politically outmaneuvered by well-organized adversaries.

In a pluralistic political system, such as the two-party democratic republic in the U.S. or multi-party system of European parliamentary democracies, organized interest groups can influence public policy by pressuring political and societal elites. Immigrant organizations, such as the National Council of La Raza, heavily promote the interests of their ethnic constituency. Ethnicity, in the words of sociologist Robert Nisbet, "is, and has been throughout history, one of the most dominant criteria of status." Nisbet argued that "[e]thnicity — broadly defined — is most likely to be the basis of caste in contrast to class in society. Even in relatively equalitarian ages, when ethnic militance and political law combine to reduce the extremer manifestations of status inequality, especially in the larger spheres of political and economic society, ethnicity continues to matter."[2] Nisbet's observation underscores the rise and influence of ethnic-immigrant interest groups in America's political system: Egalitarianism — the eradication of economic, social, and political inequalities — is the driving force behind the political activism of ethnic lobbies in the U.S. The central aim of ethnic-immigrant activism is to strip out all barriers, distinctions, and obstacles to achieve full equality.

As the population of the United States becomes ethnically more diverse, notably in the wake of the immigration reforms of the mid-1960s, ethnic-based immigrant activists have mobilized their constituency to network with other organized interest groups on the Left to influence policy decisions in the U.S. and other Western democracies. Even though ethnic-immigrant groups constitute one fraction of the greater orbit of organized lobbies (whether civic, religious, political, social, or cultural), these groups network across the social, cultural, and political divide in shoring up mutual interests (business, corporate, and labor) to advance their agenda of a world without borders.

William Hawkins and Erin Anderson, authors of *The Open Borders Lobby*, identify the ideological agenda behind the push for open borders: "The concept of 'open borders' has long been an agenda of the ideological left. Since the 1960s, a vast network including hundreds of organizations and tens of thousands of grassroots activists, backed by hundreds of millions of dollars from leftwing foundations, has waged a sustained campaign to open America's borders to a mass migration from the Third World. Though these groups talk in terms of 'human rights,' the rights they demand are not the restrictions on government enshrined in the American Bill of Rights, but the claims on society for 'equity' and 'welfare' and special treatment for designated groups that are the familiar menu of the left and would, if enacted, amount to a revolution in America's existing social order."[3]

Ethnic-immigrant lobbies serve as the radical Left's cultural beachhead. Multiculturalists—working via ethnic-immigrant advocacy groups—actively undermine America's national sovereignty and thwart the process of assimilation by breaking down traditional cultural barriers. An open-borders agenda advances the goals and objectives of ethnic-immigrant and indigenous cultures to "diversify" America's European-based heritage. The conventional idea of assimilation (adopting the values, tradition, customs, and folkways of the host nation) is now one of cultural accommodation, weaving the tapestry of the ethnic-immigrant culture into America's national fabric. Consider the transformation over the years that has taken place in the general culture with the "diversity" of languages—the often frustrating experience of encountering a voice-bank message and hearing "press 1 for English..." or going to an ATM machine and having to "press 1 for English" before proceeding with a transaction. That America continues to undergo an unprecedented demographic transition (four states now have minority-majority populations) is uncontested. What this change represents in terms of America's national interests, notably the preservation of America's national sovereignty and the nation's deeply rooted European cultural traditions, is a major focus of this book.

This chapter highlights some of the largest, most prominent ethnic-immigrant organizations pushing for open-borders and the sources of their funding.

ORGANIZED ETHNIC LOBBIES

LEAGUE OF UNITED LATIN AMERICAN CITIZENS (LULAC)

LULAC dates back to the 1920s. The first LULAC convention was held in May 1929. According to LULAC's website:

> LULAC is the largest and oldest Hispanic Organization in the United States. LULAC advances the economic condition, educational attainment, political influence, health and civil rights of Hispanic Americans through community-based programs operating at more than 700 LULAC councils nationwide. The organization involves and serves all Hispanic nationality groups.
>
> Historically, LULAC has focused heavily on education, civil rights, and employment for Hispanics. LULAC councils provide more than a million dollars in scholarships to Hispanic students each year, conduct citizenship and voter registration drives, develop low income housing units, conduct youth leadership training programs, and seek to empower the Hispanic community at the local, state and national level.
>
> In addition, the LULAC National Educational Service Centers, LULAC's educational arm, provides counseling services to more than 18,000 Hispanic students per year at sixteen regional centers. SER Jobs for Progress, LULAC's employment arm, provides job skills and literacy training to the Hispanic community through more than forty-eight employment training centers located throughout the United States. The LULAC Corporate Alliance, an advisory board of Fortune 500

8

companies, fosters stronger partnerships between Corporate America and the Hispanic community.

LULAC's success in attaining major funding for its various projects is evident in this abstract of an article from *The Hispanic Outlook in Higher Education*:

> The AT&T Foundation, philanthropic arm of AT&T Inc., and the League of United Latin American Citizens (LULAC) have unveiled 32 locations that will house new community technology centers in low-income Hispanic communities through LULAC's Empower Hispanic America with Technology initiative. The centers are being supported by a $1.5 million grant that builds on the success of the foundation's $1 million grant to LULAC in 2004. "In addition to creating 32 new technology centers, the funds will also enable us to maintain 23 current locations established under the previous grant," said LULAC National President Rosa Rosales. "More than 55,000 Latinos received access and instruction on computer technology through AT&T's support in 2004. And we expect this new grant to more than double the number of people we can help." The grant to LULAC is part of AT&T AccessAll, a three-year $100 million philanthropic initiative to provide technology access to underserved communities. It will provide each new facility with computer equipment, personnel support, high-speed Internet service, and videoconferencing.

LULAC recently announced a "partnership" with Tyson Foods (a company once indicted on charges of smuggling illegal alien workers into the U.S.) to assist "the hungry in the Latino community" by setting up a food bank network in San Antonio, Texas. Tyson's latest donations of 15 tons of protein to the San Antonio Food Bank bring the total in-kind donations (since 2000) to over 50 million pounds or 200 million meals.

Comcast recently partnered with LULAC to launch "Our Time to Vote," a year-long effort to campaign for voter education and registration in Hispanic communities. This $5 million "multicultural outreach" campaign is part of Comcast's overall commitment to "diversity" in four key areas: "attracting and retaining a multicultural workforce, developing a diverse supplier group, offering a wide selection of multicultural programming and pledging significant community investments."

"'Our Time to Vote' is designed to bring a wide range of diverse Americans into the voting process," explained Susan Gonzales, corporate senior director of federal and external affairs and vice president of the Comcast Foundation.

NATIONAL COUNCIL OF LA RAZA (NCLR)

The National Council of La Raza (NCLR), founded in 1968, is a nonprofit advocacy organization based in Washington, D.C., La Raza (or "the race") maintains a network of 300 affiliate "community-based organizations" throughout the United States. Early on the Ford Foundation provided substantial funding that was instrumental to La Raza's founding and growth over the years. Other recent corporate "partners" include: Johnson & Johnson; Bank of America; PepsiCo, Inc.; Citi; Wal-Mart Stores, Inc.; State Farm Insurance Companies; Comcast Communications; and Verizon.

Raul Humberto Yzaguirre, born in San Juan, Texas in 1939, served as president of La Raza from 1974-2004 and now works with several nonprofit organizations as an advocate for creating a political union between Mexico, Canada, and the United States. Yzaguirre is a lifetime member of the Council on Foreign Relations and served on the Independent Task Force on North America, which published *Building a North America Community* and called for greater cooperation in the free movement of commerce, capital, and people in a North American union. La Raza's headquarter building in Washington, D.C. is named after Yzaguirre.

Wikipedia.com summarizes the activities, goals, and objectives of the NCLR:

> NCLR works on a variety of different issues
> affecting the Latino community in the U.S. such

10

as health, housing, education, workforce development, and youth leadership. NCLR's Institute for Hispanic Health works to reduce the incidence, burden, and impact of health conditions such as diabetes, heart disease, cancer, and HIV/AIDS. The NCLR Homeownership Network operates in 20 states and provides counseling on purchasing a home and managing the investment after purchase. NCLR also has both early childhood and secondary education programs which stress literacy, college preparation, and parent involvement. The organization's education programs also address the needs of Latino and English-language-learner students through a network of community-based charter schools. In addition, NCLR works to increase employment opportunities for Latino youth through its *Escalera* program. Youth leadership is also stressed in the *Líderes* initiative that links youth development organizations around the country into one national network. Through all these programs, NCLR provides technical assistance to its network of community-based organizations around the country working on the same issues.

NCLR's policy team also works on a range of similar issues including civic engagement, criminal and juvenile justice, wealth-building, housing, education, health, and that for which they are most well-known, immigration. The organization ***advocates on behalf of Hispanics in the United States*** by conducting research and ***informing policy-makers about how proposed or existing legislation affects the Latino community.***[4] [Emphasis added.]

Moreover, the NCLR website describes its mission, namely to conduct "applied research, policy analysis, and advocacy, providing a Latino perspective in five key areas — assets/investments, civil rights/immigration, education, employment

11

and economic status, and health. In addition, it provides capacity-building assistance to its Affiliates who work at the state and local level to advance opportunities for individuals and families."

NATIONAL LATINO CONGRESO (NLC)

The National Latino Congreso (NLC) is an affiliate of the William C. Velasquez Institute (WCVI). The Velasquez Institute works "to conduct research into improving the level of political and economic participation in Latino and other underrepresented communities." The NLC serves as an umbrella support group coordinating and consolidating the heads of the major organizations representing ethnic-immigrant causes. The purpose of the NLC was to coordinate the activities of leading Latino organizations in stopping "anti-immigration" efforts (translation: tougher border security, protecting America's national sovereignty, preserving America's European cultural traditions, and deporting illegal aliens). The following organizations comprise the NLC:

- ◄ Hispanic Federation (HF) — hispanicfederation.org
- ◄ Labor Council for Latin American Advancement (LCLAA) — lclaa.org
- ◄ League of United Latin American Citizens (LULAC) — lulac.org
- ◄ Mexican American Legal Defense and Educational Fund (MALDEF) — maldef.org
- ◄ National Alliance of Latin American and Caribbean Communities (NALACC) — nalacc.org
- ◄ National Day Laborer Organizing Network (NDLON) — ndlon.org
- ◄ National Hispanic Environmental Council (NHEC) — nheec.org
- ◄ Southwest Voter Registration Education Project (SVREP) — svrep.org
- ◄ William C. Velasquez Institute (WCVI) — wcvi.org

Previous sponsors (providing financial support or goods and services) of NLC include:

- Southwest Airlines
- General Motors
- Starbucks
- Sierra Club
- Levi Strauss Foundation
- Wells Fargo
- Whole Foods
- Union Bank of California
- Charles R. Drew University of Medicine and Science
- The Nature Conservancy
- Oxfam America
- Titan
- Nielsen
- Sempra Energy

MEXICAN AMERICAN LEGAL DEFENSE AND EDUCATIONAL FUND (MALDEF)

Another major ethnic-immigrant advocacy organization is the Mexican American Legal Defense and Educational Fund (MALDEF). Founded in 1968 in San Antonio, Texas, MALDEF claims it is the "leading Latino litigation, advocacy, and educational outreach institution in the U.S." The primary mission of MALDEF is to "foster sound public policies, laws, and programs to safeguard the civil rights of the 45 million Latinos living in the United States and to empower the Latino community to fully participate in our society." MALDEF received the financial support of a $2.2 million grant from the Ford Foundation in 1968. It maintains several regional offices and a staff of 50 employees and 22 attorneys. The 25-member board of directors is comprised of leaders from the public and private sector, government, and law firms. Headquartered in Los Angeles, MALDEF has won several significant legal victories for Mexican Americans in lawsuits over voting rights, employment discrimination, educational funding, and access to public education for the children of illegal aliens.

Corporate sponsors (corporate and foundation partners)

who have contributed over $100,000 include:

◄ Anheuser-Busch companies

◄ Ford Foundation

◄ Rockefeller Foundation

◄ Soros Foundation

◄ Washington Mutual Bank

NATIONAL IMMIGRANT
SOLIDARITY NETWORK (NISN)

According to the National Immigrant Solidarity Network (NISN) website, the NISN is "a coalition of immigrant rights, labor, human rights, religious, and student activist organizations from across the country." In solidarity with their campaigns, the NISN assists in organizing community immigrant rights education campaigns.

> From legislative letter-writing campaigns to speaker bureaus and educational materials, we organize critical immigrant-worker campaigns that are moving toward justice for all immigrants!

MOVIMIENTO ESTUDIANTIL
CHICANO DE AZTLÁN (MEChA)

MEChA is a self-described "Chicano" student organization and wraps itself in the language of "liberation," "self-determination," and "struggle" of "Indigenous people." The MEChA website explains the orientation, background, and objectives of the Chicano student organization:

> Movimiento Estudiantil Chicano de Aztlán (MEChA) is a student organization that promotes higher education, cultura, and historia. MEChA was founded on the principles of self-determination for the liberation of our people. We believe that political involvement and education is the avenue for change in our society.
>
> Each word in MEChA symbolizes a great concept in terms of la causa. Movimiento means that the organization is dedicated to the movement to

gain self-determination for our people. Estudiantil, identifies the organization as a student group for we are part of our Raza's future. At the heart of the name is the use of the identity: Chicano. At first seen as a negative word, now taken for a badge of honor. In adopting their new identity, the students committed themselves to return to the barrios, colonias, or campos and together, struggle against the forces that oppress our gente. Lastly, the affirmation that we are Indigenous people to this land by placing our movement in Aztlan, the homeland of all peoples from Anahuak.

On campuses across Aztlan, MEChA and Mechistas are often the only groups on campus Raza and non-Raza alike that seek to open the doors of higher education para nuestras comunidades and strive for a society free of imperialism, racism, sexism, and homophobia. An inspirational statement in El Plan Santa Barbara that speaks to this notes:

"MEChA must bring to the mind of every young Chicana and Chicano that the liberation of her/his people from prejudice and oppression is in her/his hands and this responsibility is greater than personal achievement and more meaningful than degrees, especially if they are earned at the expense of her/his identity and cultural integrity. MEChA, then, is more than a name; it is a spirit of unity, of sisterhood and brotherhood, and a resolve to undertake a struggle for liberation in society where justice is but a word. MEChA is a means to an end" (El Plan de Santa Barbara).

Historical Foundation

In March of 1969, at Denver, Colorado the Crusade for Justice organized the first National Chicano Youth Liberation Conference that drafted the basic premises for the Chicana/Chicano Movement in El Plan de Aztlán.

The following month, in April of 1969, over 100 Chicanas/Chicanos came together at the University of California, Santa Barbara to formulate a plan for higher education: El Plan de Santa Barbara. With this document they were successful in the development of two very important contributions to the Chicano Movement: Movimiento Estudiantil Chicano de Aztlán (MEChA) and Chicano Studies.

The adoption of the name Movimiento Estudiantil Chicano de Aztlan signaled a new level of political consciousness among student activists. It was the final stage in the transformation of what had been loosely organized, local student groups, into a single structure and a unified student movement.

Adamant rejection of the label "Mexican-American" meant rejection of the assimilation and accommodationist melting pot ideology that had guided earlier generations of activists. Chicanismo involves a crucial distinction in a political consciousness between a Mexican-American (Hispanic) and a Chicana/o mentality. El Plan de Santa Barbara speaks to such issues of identity politics by asserting:

"The Mexican-American (Hispanic) is a person who lacks respect for his/her cultural and ethnic heritage. Unsure of her/himself, she/he seeks assimilation as a way out of her/his "degraded" social status. Consequently, she/he remains politically ineffective. In contrast, Chicanismo reflects self-respect and pride on one's ethnic and cultural background. Thus, the Chicana/o acts with confidence and with a range of alternatives in the political world. She/he is capable of developing an effective ideology through action" (El Plan de Santa Barbara).

MEChA played an important role in the creation and implementation of Chicana/o Studies and support services programs on campus. Chicana/o Studies programs would be a relevant alternative to established curricula. Most important, the Chicana/o Studies program would be the foundation of MEChA's political power base. Today many Chicana/os [sic] Studies Programs would have difficulty operating if it were not for the enthusiasm and dedication of Mechistas to Chicana/o Studies.

DeleteTheBorder.org

One of the more radical operations pushing for openborders is a consortium of militant-Left activists working to advance "direct democracy" and "direct action" as well as championing "indigenous struggles" and "immigrant rights" is DeleteTheBorder.org. According to its website,

Deletetheborder.org is an online community with the goal of nurturing a global network of movements against borders. We began the project in 2005. Sensing the tremendous potential energy and having seen the existence of many networks around the world like NoBorder.org and No One Is Illegal in Canada, we sought to use the latest technology to provide a site which would make international connections and act as a hub of resistance and emergence.

Deletetheborder.org is designed to be a place for information sharing through the use of open posting, news feed collection, media galleries, blogs and forums. We are currently in the midst of the largest migration in human history. The intense processes of neoliberal enclosure continue on despite unprecedented levels of resistance across the world. Thus, migration continues, from South to North, from colonized to colonizer. Most recently, under the guise of the war on terror, States are retaliating against this migration with repressive measures and elaborate systems of control and exploitation that function much like in-country colonization.

Against this murderous violence, movements have sprung up to work in conjunction and solidarity with migrant people. Our site seeks to aid the growth of these movements by providing information about borders and resistance to borders, but also by providing support for organizers including forums, hosting for data sharing and event calendars.

Our site currently offers visitors the option to see the site's interface elements such as menus and buttons in English, Spanish or French. It also allows visitors to post translations for their stories. We frequently have posts in each of these languages as the posts often originate in the US, Canada, Mexico and Spain. Our contexts are some of the most contentious and violent borderlands of the world.

The project was begun, and is maintained by the o.r.g.a.n.i.c. collective and the borderlands hacklab in San Diego, California. The content of Deletetheborder.org is contributed by numerous organizers, hackers and bloggers in the US, Canada and Mexico. Stories are regularly posted by members of o.r.g.a.n.i.c, by organizers with No One Is Illegal in Canada and by net activists such as Ricardo Dominguez. Moving forward, the o.r.g.a.n.i.c collective and the borderlands Hacklab is working on a more formalized North American Network For Freedom of Movement. The administration of the site therefore, will soon include members of various groups around the country, including the Bay Area Coalition to Fight the Minutemen.

Within the last month our site traffic has doubled as the largest mobilizations ever seen in many cities across the US have taken place, including self-organized spontaneous walkouts by tens of thousands of students.

PHILANTHROPIC SUPPORT:
FOUNDATIONS FUNDING THE OPEN-BORDERS NETWORK

THE FORD FOUNDATION

Over the years, large private foundations have bankrolled organizations such as the Mexican American Legal Defense and Educational Fund (MALDEF). Chief among the

Wealthiest Foundations (25 largest charitable non-profits worldwide)			
1. Bill & Melinda Gates Foundation	United States	Seattle, WA	$38.7 billion
2. Wellcome Trust	United Kingdom	London	$23.2 billion
3. Howard Hughes Medical Institute	United States	Chevy Chase, MD	$18.6 billion
4. Ford Foundation	United States	New York, NY	$13.7 billion
5. The Church Commissioners for England	United Kingdom	London	$10.5 billion
6. J. Paul Getty Trust	United States	Los Angeles, CA	$10.1 billion
7. Li Ka Shing Foundation	Hong Kong	Hong Kong	$10.0 billion
8. Robert Wood Johnson Foundation	United States	Princeton, NJ	$10.0 billion
9. William & Flora Hewlett Foundation	United States	Menlo Park, CA	$8.5 billion
10. W. K. Kellogg Foundation	United States	Battle Creek, MI	$8.4 billion
11. Lilly Endowment	United States	Indianapolis, IN	$7.6 billion
12. Garfield Weston Foundation	United Kingdom	London	$6.9 billion
13. Robert Bosch Foundation	Germany	Stuttgart	$6.9 billion
14. David & Lucile Packard Foundation	United States	Los Altos	$6.3 billion
15. Andrew W. Mellon Foundation	United States	New York, NY	$6.1 billion
16. John D. & Catherine T. MacArthur Foundation	United States	Chicago, IL	$6.1 billion
17. Gordon E. & Betty I. Moore Foundation	United States	San Francisco, CA	$5.8 billion
18. Realdania	Denmark	Copenhagen	$5.6 billion
19. Knut & Alice Wallenberg Foundation	Sweden	Stockholm	$5.3 billion
20. The California Endowment	United States	Los Angeles, CA	$4.4 billion
21. The Pew Charitable Trusts	United States	Philadelphia, PA	$4.1 billion
22. Calouste Gulbenkian Foundation	Portugal	Lisbon	$3.8 billion
23. Rockefeller Foundation	United States	New York, NY	$3.8 billion
24. The Starr Foundation	United States	New York, NY	$3.5 billion
25. The Kresge Foundation	United States	Detroit, MI	$3.3 billion

*Source: http://n.wikipedia.org/wiki/List_of_wealthiest_foundations

foundations funding MALDEF and other ethnic-immigrant groups is the Ford Foundation.

The Ford Foundation was chartered in 1936 by Michigan philanthropist Edsel Bryant Ford. Edsel Ford, the son of Henry Ford, is a former president of Ford Motor Company. The Ford Foundation is an independent philanthropic organization with no present direct affiliation with the Ford Motor Company (Henry Ford II resigned from the Ford Foundation board of directors in 1976). Originally the foundation was established to fund Henry Ford's philanthropic vision and priorities.

The Ford Foundation is listed as the third largest charitable foundation in the U.S., coming in behind the Bill and Melinda Gates Foundation and the Howard Hughes Medical Institute (see chart on page 19). With an endowment of $13.7 billion, the Ford Foundation is a major financial supporter of "those on the margins of social, economic and political life." The Ford Foundation website describes their mission:

> As citizens, we each have a central role to play in fulfilling the promises of peace and social justice in our societies. We support civic groups because we believe they provide a key platform enabling people to share in charting the future of their communities and defending against the abuse of public or private power.
>
> Our work in this area expands opportunities for people around the world to build and sustain civic life in ways that promote peaceful and just communities. We concentrate on strengthening the organizations, networks and movements through which people exercise citizenship. We also encourage voluntary associations to hold themselves and their governments accountable for their actions.

Key Strategies

Our grant making focuses on:

◁ Helping grassroots groups, nonprofits and membership organizations articulate common

20

goals, strengthen their capacities and account-ability, and build alliances with government and business

◄ Strengthening philanthropy that gives voice to those on the margins of social, economic and political life

◄ Promoting greater civic engagement in the institutions of global governance

We believe that a healthy civil society relies on a critical mass of people and organizations work-ing in a variety of ways on common challenges. Our grants place emphasis on collaboration and continual learning about best practices in differ-ing contexts around the world.

THE OPEN SOCIETY INSTITUTE (OSI)

The mission of the Open Society Institute (OSI), a private-operating and grant-making foundation, "aims to shape public policy to promote democratic governance, human rights, and economic, legal, and social reform. On a local level, OSI imple-ments a range of initiatives to support the rule of law, educa-tion, public health, and independent media. At the same time, OSI works to build alliances across borders and continents on issues such as combating corruption and rights abuses."

OSI has launched some 33 global and local initiatives that span the full range of anti-poverty, human rights, health, cultural, women's rights, and social justice issues in the con-text of a borderless world.[5]

Between 1996-2000, OSI sponsored the Emma Lazarus Fund, which "focused on combating the unfair treatment of immigrants in the United States. In its final year, it was the lead funder of the Los Angeles Immigrant Funders' Collaborative, which provides grants to nonprofit orga-nizations that support the needs of immigrant and refu-gee communities in the areas of health care, education, civic participation, and economic development."[6]

An *Investor's Business Daily* editorial in September 2007 raised the irony of the lack of "transparency" in which OSI funded various public projects:

> Didn't the mainstream media report that 2006's vast immigration rallies across the country began as a spontaneous uprising of 2 million angry Mexican-flag waving illegal immigrants demanding U.S. citizenship in Los Angeles, egged on only by a local Spanish-language radio announcer?
>
> Turns out that wasn't what happened, either. Soros' OSI had money-muscle there, too, through its $17 million Justice Fund. The fund lists 19 projects in 2006. One was vaguely described involvement in the immigration rallies. Another project funded illegal immigrant activist groups for subsequent court cases.
>
> So what looked like a wildfire grassroots movement really was a manipulation from OSI's glassy Manhattan offices. The public had no way of knowing until the release of OSI's 2006 annual report.... Soros' "shaping public policies," as OSI calls it, is not illegal. But it's a problem for democracy because it drives issues with cash and then only lets the public know about it after it's old news.
>
> That means the public makes decisions about issues without understanding the special agendas of groups behind them.
>
> Without more transparency, it amounts to political manipulation. This leads to cynicism. As word of these short-term covert ops gets out, the public grows to distrust what it hears and tunes out.
>
> The irony here is that Soros claims to be an advocate of an "open society." His OSI does just the legal minimum to disclose its activities. The public shouldn't have to wait until an annual report is out before the light is flipped on about the Open Society's political action.[7]

The organizations listed above form the tip of the ethnic

advocacy groups in the open-borders network. In seeking a borderless society — a multicultural, multi-ethnic America that would be unrecognizable to generations of descendants of our nation's European settlers — these ethnic-immigrant lobbies aggressively promote a borderless society. As these radical groups gain additional support and ultimately wield further political leverage, Middle America will be eclipsed by well-managed, well-funded, highly-organized ethnic groups actively "changing" American society to the detriment of the national interest.

Endnotes

1. Garrett Hardin, *Stalking the Wild Taboo*, 2nd ed. (Los Altos, CA: William Kaufmann, Inc., 1978: 206).
2. Robert A. Nisbet, *The Social Bond: An Introduction to the Study of Society* (New York: Alfred A. Knopf, 1970: 193).
3. William Hawkins and Erin Anderson, *The Open Borders Lobby and the Nation's Security After 9/11* (Los Angeles, CA: Center for the Study of Popular Culture, 2004: 11).
4. http://en.wikipedia.org/wiki/National_Council_of_La_Raza
5. http://www.soros.org/initiatives
6. http://www.soros.org/about/overview/z_past_initiatives/list
7. "The Soros Threat to Democracy," *Investor's Business Daily*, September 25, 2007: A12.

2

THE POLITICAL SPHERE

કેન્જ

THE PROBLEM OF UNCONTROLLED immigration, above all from the Third World, is no longer confined to a handful of states like California, New York, Texas, Florida, and a few big cities. Today, thanks to the continued failure of America's political leaders to secure our borders, aliens — illegal and otherwise — willing to work for low wages are crowding Americans out of the workforce from Maine to Hawaii. Americans in the heartland, burdened by the costs of war and economic slump, have in recent years been bearing the additional expense of welfare for aliens, including those here unlawfully. Across the nation, its citizens must contend with imported challenges to America's traditional majority language, religion, customs, and standards of public health and safety. Most threatening of all, America's immigrant population contains high numbers of criminals as well as many more of the politically and religiously aggrieved from whose numbers the attackers of 9/11 and other terrorist incidents were recruited.

No group bears a greater responsibility for America's open borders than the nation's elected officials. After all, they have sworn to uphold the nation's laws, and it is their pledged duty to defend the security and protect the welfare of their constituents, the American people. Yet shockingly many of our political leaders have refused to enforce even the duly enacted laws that shield our borders and our workplaces against illegal entry and illegal competition from abroad.

After America's traditional immigration policy was altered to allow massive immigration from Africa, Asia, and Latin America during Lyndon Johnson's liberal "Great Society," successive American presidents and legislators chose to stand pat. With a handful of honorable exceptions, the nation's elected leaders have sought only to expand opportunities for foreigners to immigrate to America. Now, despite the attacks of 9/11, and despite the worsening fortunes of working- and middle-class Americans, the nation's political leadership continues not only to tolerate the present immigrant flood but to demand and to enable more legal immigrants and to offer amnesty to aliens here illegally.

From the White House and the Capitol to all too many statehouses and city halls, our elected executives and lawmakers have ignored the desire of the great majority of the electorate that they secure the nation's borders, enforce the laws against illegal entrants, and bring immigration under control.

Their refusal to do so defies easy categories of party or political philosophy. Supporters of providing amnesty for illegal aliens, of importing ever more immigrants legally, and of increasing welfare benefits for legal and illegal entrants have included America's Republican and professedly conservative president; major presidential contenders; the Democratic Congressional leadership; powerful senators and representatives; and the governors, both Democratic and Republican, of influential states as well as the mayors of many of America's leading cities.

NEGLECT IN THE WHITE HOUSE

The failure to secure the nation's borders and to protect the weal of the American people against a flood of cheap labor, imported crime and disease, and alien mores starts at the top with President George W. Bush. Despite the President's Republican and conservative credentials, his record on immigration has arguably been worse than that of his predecessor,

Bill Clinton. President Bush pressed for amnesty to twelve or more million illegal aliens, the most extravagant in U.S. history. He championed the interests of business against those of American workers by permitting unprecedented neglect of workplace enforcement of immigration laws and by advocating the admission of vast numbers of foreigners for employment in American industry.

Even before his election in 2000, Bush, who as governor of Texas billed himself as a "compassionate conservative," opposed efforts to outlaw state welfare for illegals and pushed for costly bilingual education, which retards pupils' ability to gain fluency in English for immigrant children. [1]

During the 2000 election campaign, at a time when illegal immigration was flourishing under the presidency of Bill Clinton, Bush summed up his views on protecting our borders by stating that "immigration is not a problem to be solved, it is a sign of a successful nation."[2]

In that campaign, Bush again expressed support for bilingual education and also espoused "English-plus." This program gives lip service to requiring newcomers to learn America's language but if enacted would entitle them to use a multiplicity of other languages in government offices, the courts, and hospital emergency rooms, while requiring taxpayers to pay for their translators.[3]

The attacks of 9/11, carried out by immigrants several of whom were here illegally, were by no means the wake-up call for the Bush administration on immigration they should have been. Bush responded to the devastation inflicted by the alien hijackers not with a hardened determination to enforce national laws already on the books against those who enter, stay, and work in America illegally, but rather with an offer of amnesty.

On January 8, 2004, President Bush announced to a group of "Latino" leaders visiting the White House that he supported legislation to grant six years of legal status to some eight million illegal aliens. Thereafter he has backed a succession of Congressional bills aimed at "comprehensive immigration reform," each of which has offered the equivalent of amnesty to the great majority of the unlawful immigrants (recently estimated at over twelve million) within our borders.[4]

In 2006, the President supported the Comprehensive Immigration Reform Act (U.S. Senate Bill 2611), which, unlike a competing bill drawn up by Republican leaders in the House, would have allowed some ten million illegal aliens to apply for and receive offered amnesty.[5]

When that bill failed, despite support from powerful ethnic, corporate, and other institutional interests, due to the massive opposition of ordinary Americans, President Bush supported the misnamed Secure Borders, Economic Opportunity, and Immigration Reform Act of 2007 (S. 1348), which would have made amnesty available to even more illegal entrants.[6] Despite the defeat of that bill, too, President Bush continued to advocate "a path to citizenship" for the vast majority of the millions who have violated the nation's borders.

Nearly five years after 9/11, President Bush acknowledged that he had yet to abolish the shameful "catch and release" practice whereby immigration enforcement authorities have allowed countless thousands of aliens who have been detained, many of them for additional crimes, to be released from custody with summonses for hearings for which they never show up.[7]

President Bush has made it abundantly clear he is more concerned about the desires of American business for cheap and tractable immigrant workers than the needs of the American people for secure borders, economic well-being, and cultural stability. In his 2006 State of the Union address, he told the nation that America's economy could not function without immigrants.[8] Two years earlier, in his 2004 State of the Union address, the President revealed an even more striking plan for the national economy: he called for a "new temporary-worker program to match willing foreign workers with willing employers when no Americans can be found to fill the job." This vision regards the United States of America as one great hiring hall in which American workers must compete for jobs with foreigners willing and able to work for far less pay and far fewer benefits, thereby swelling corporate earnings. It is, of course, a vision shared by much of American business.

While Bush has courted the votes of ethnic blocs supportive of amnesty, he has been even more dependent on corporate support stemming from his backing for an array of immigration programs that have brought millions of foreigners to America during his tenure to take jobs in agriculture, medicine, the computer industry, and as business executives.[9] And, as might have been predicted, during George Bush's presidency enforcement of immigration laws against employers who hire illegals has become negligible—indeed, well beneath enforcement levels under the immigration-friendly President Bill Clinton.

THE CANDIDATES: PLEDGED TO AMNESTY

Unfortunately, President Bush's policy has not been an aberration. His calls to "stay the course" in encouraging out-of-control legal immigration and his actions in tolerating and privileging illegal immigrants have been echoed—and sometimes exceeded—by leading Democrats and Republicans, from the presidential candidates on down.

Despite lip service to securing our borders, then Senator Hillary Clinton (D-NY) had strongly supported George Bush's "path to legalization" (none dare call it amnesty!) for the millions of unlawful aliens already here.[10] She has consistently voted for amnesty legislation that would have done just that and has promised to introduce legislation to achieve this during the first hundred days of her presidency.[11]

Senator Clinton is opposed to state and local law enforcement officials inquiring about immigration status (although thousands of serious crimes have been later committed by illegals who could have been deported earlier). She tolerates "sanctuary cities," those enclaves whose mayors have ordered police and other city officials to ignore federal immigration laws. She has also voted against penalizing those who knowingly assist illegal aliens to violate immigration laws.[12]

Her Senate voting record includes ayes for unlawful immigrants receiving Social Security benefits and for Medicaid for underage resident aliens. Like President Bush, she

29

opposes making English America's official language, despite the vast tangible and intangible costs of the linguistic balkanizing of America—although she has conceded that "English does remain an important part of the American experience."[13]

While he was in the U.S. Senate, Barack Obama (D-IL), for all his mantra of hope and change, has given little hope that he would change immigration law and enforcement—for the better, anyway. The proud son of an immigrant from Kenya, Senator Obama backed the Bush amnesty for illegals and supported increased legal immigration by "keeping families together" (i.e., importing relatives of families already here).[14]

Obama claims that the immigration crisis is the result not of America's political leaders selling out to special interests, but of a "dysfunctional bureaucracy;" he has accordingly introduced the Citizenship Promotion Act, which would make it cheaper for aliens to apply for citizenship, and despite the criminal and security risks, pressure the FBI to make much speedier background checks of applicants for citizenship.[15] Thus it will come as no surprise that Obama favors arming illegal aliens with state-issued driver's licenses, opposes efforts by state governments to deny them welfare, has supported Medicaid for illegal minors, and rejects making English the nation's official language.[16]

Despite the aura of patriotism and devotion to national security that stems from his military career, John McCain's position on immigration is best exemplified by his coauthorship with Senator Ted Kennedy (D-MA) of the so-called "Secure America and Orderly Immigration Act." According to one respected immigration research group, that bill (S. 1033) was "amnesty legislation on a massive, historically unprecedented scale."[17]

Senator McCain, who said in 2004, "Everybody in the world should have the opportunity through an orderly process to come to this country," has been advocating what in effect are open borders for some time.[18]

In 2000, McCain supported the Latino and Immigrant Fairness Act, which, he later admitted, made "progress on amnesty for those wrongly denied it," including persons here illegally from Haiti and several Central American countries.[19] Sanctimoniously proclaiming that "we need…to recognize these are God's children as well," McCain has voted to allow illegal immigrants to receive Social Security benefits from work done here illegally. He opposes making English America's official language and opposed Arizona's 2004 Proposition 200, which sought to limit public benefits to citizens.[20]

Following grassroots opposition to the several different amnesty measures he supported, Senator McCain has sought to remake himself as a champion of border security, voting for the Secure Fence Act of 2006 and advocating for rounding up and deporting the estimated *two million* unlawful entrants who have committed additional crimes since breaching our borders.[21]

Senator McCain's impersonation of an enemy of open borders is less than convincing. During a presidential debate in New Hampshire in 2007, he stated that the mere presence of twelve million aliens here illegally constituted "de facto amnesty." That kind of wish-fulfillment, and the sleight of hand whereby McCain hopes that rewarding those and other illegals with official amnesty will deter additional waves of unlawful entrants, should be enough to alert citizens to the sad truth that there is essentially no difference between Hillary Clinton, Barack Obama, and John McCain when it comes to the presidential duty of guarding America's borders.[22]

A CONGRESS INCREASINGLY ALIENATED FROM AMERICANS

In 2006 and 2007, citizen opposition to President Bush's amnesty proposal derailed Congressional bills aimed at enacting it. Yet the leaders of both parties on Capitol Hill, eager to attract corporate largesse and electoral support from immigrant-ethnic and racial blocs, continue to work toward amnesty, increased legal immigration, and other open-border goals.

Thus Senate majority leader Harry Reid (D-NV) supported President Bush's "path toward citizenship" for border breakers. He sponsored a bill that would have allowed the families of amnestied illegals and large numbers of legal immigrant workers to join them in this country.[23] He voted against enhanced security measures, including a fence, along America's border with Mexico. To make things sweeter for future arrivals from abroad, legal or illegal, he has supported Social Security benefits for illegal workers and, in 1997, voted in favor of food stamps for illegal aliens. Senator Reid has supported increased immigration of foreign workers, skilled and agricultural, and has voted against making English the official language of the U.S.[24]

Senator Richard Durbin (D-IL), the Senate majority whip (charged with mustering quorums and maintaining party discipline), largely echoes Reid's open-borders stance and if anything has been more profligate. Not only has Senator Durbin voted for Medicaid for illegal aliens' children, in 2007, he introduced the bizarre Development, Relief and Education for Alien Minors (DREAM) Act. If passed, the DREAM Act has the potential to grant citizenship to potentially hundreds of thousands of illegal alien students — and their parents.[25]

While not all the Democratic rank and file has voted with Reid, Durbin, and the totemic Senator Edward Kennedy (D-MA), a leading figure in the drive to destroy America's traditional border safeguards for over forty years, Democrats in the House and Senate have generally followed their leaders in undermining immigration control. Despite her lofty position, House Speaker Nancy Pelosi (D-CA) is typical: she supports amnesty; opposes the border security fence; voted against requiring hospitals to report treating illegal aliens as a condition of federal reimbursement; backed extending immigrant residency; and voted aye to more immigrant visas for skilled workers.[26]

The posture of the Senate's Republican leadership exemplifies the contradictions of the GOP's position on immigration control. The Republicans' constituents reject amnesty and increasingly opposed the Bush administration's efforts to expand legal immigration. The wealth and power that America's industrial, financial, media, and educational establishment have deployed to court GOP legislators, however, coupled with occasional efforts to compete with Democrats for the votes of Latinos and other immigrant blocs, has resulted at best in holding the line against blanket amnesty and beating back the more outrageous attempts to reward and privilege immigrants at the expense of Americans.

Thus, Senate minority leader Mitch McConnell (R-KY) voted in favor of an amnesty bill in 2006 but, up for re-election in 2008, voted against the comprehensive amnesty act of 2007 (S. 1348). He has consistently supported importing foreign "guest workers," skilled and unskilled, and voted to expand their numbers.[27] Minority whip John Kyl (R-AZ), like John McCain from a border state that has been flooded with illegal aliens from Mexico, together with his fellow senator opposed Arizona's Proposition 200, an effort to deny state benefits to the illegals who were burdening its educational and medical systems. Kyl supported the McCain-Kennedy amnesty bill and has gratified his state's business establishment by voting for visas for foreign agricultural and technical workers in large numbers.[28]

No less a conservative mainstay than Trent Lott (R-MI) has supported the president's amnesty program,[29] while even Senator Larry Craig, from highly conservative Idaho, has voted for amnesty and greatly increased legal immigration and opposed construction of the border fence. Acutely attuned to the desires of his state's agribusiness, he has stated of illegal farm workers: "They're all here, and they're necessary."[30]

Against legislative colleagues from their party who find themselves torn between patriotic duty and corporate blandishments, as well as those who unreservedly embrace open borders, immigration-control stalwarts like Representatives James Sensenbrenner (R-WI) and Tom Tancredo (R-CO) have done well indeed to hold the line on amnesty. But unless they are heavily reinforced, and soon, secure borders and American standards of employment may become a thing of the past.

RELUCTANT DEFENDERS, OPEN ABETTORS

Traditionally America's governors have left enforcing

America's immigration laws to the federal government. In recent years, however, the impact of migrants from abroad, legal and illegal, has tempted several governors to court immigrant support by offering benefits and privileges. In several states, however, an aroused electorate has rejected such efforts. California's Democratic Governor Gray Davis's approval of a bill to award driver's licenses to illegal aliens, which of course serve as effective identification documents anywhere in America, was a key factor in his removal from office by voter recall in 2003.[31] Even before his recent disgrace, New York's former Democratic Governor Eliot Spitzer squandered a considerable amount of his 2006 landslide electoral backing through his own plan to help legalize the illegal by issuing them driver's licenses, and he was forced to abandon it in late 2007.[32]

Emblematic of the effects of growing citizen opposition to uncontrolled immigration, particularly in our border states, has been the recent career of Arizona's Democratic Governor Janet Napolitano. Governor Napolitano vociferously opposed Arizona's Proposition 200 in 2004. Two years after opposing that measure to deny state benefits to unlawful immigrants, the Governor was forced to call out the National Guard to protect Arizona's border, and later she signed legislation to penalize employers who knowingly hire illegal aliens.[33]

Whatever impetus the out-of-control immigration situation lends to control efforts at the state level, it seems to fizzle out in America's cities, particularly the large ones. In many of these, the massive presence of recent immigrants, legal and illegal, has encouraged an effort by mayors to proclaim their jurisdictions as "sanctuary cities," that is, places where municipal employees defy federal immigration laws by mayoral order. Such cities not only include New York, Los Angeles, San Francisco, and Phoenix, but also Portland (Maine), Salt Lake City, and Washington, DC. The motivations of Los Angeles's mayor, Antonio Villaraigosa, to support his Mexican coethnics on both sides of the border (in college he was a member of MEChA, a group that calls for reconquering much of the U.S. for Mexico), may transcend the purely venal.

But what of the motives—and the loyalties—of the mayors of the dozens of cities now offering "sanctuary" to several million violators of our laws and our borders?[34]

A FLAWED BELIEF SYSTEM

How did America's traditional immigration policy come to be abandoned, and the nation's borders opened to millions of Third World immigrants, during a little over four decades during which demonstrably patriotic, and for the most part conservative, Republican Presidents have led the country? To be sure, Democratic congressional majorities, liberal court rulings, and bureaucratic lag and drag have hindered efforts at immigration control. Yet political interest—in opposing an influx of potential voters economically and ethnically linked to the Democratic base—as well as civic duty could have been expected to produce far stronger Republican opposition to what has been unchecked immigration, coupled with half a dozen previous amnesties to illegal aliens, since 1986.

One answer to the question of why Republicans and conservatives have tolerated or even enabled open borders lies in the rise of an ideology that embraces economic growth, to be achieved by free trade, open markets, and open borders, above all other values. New York's Mayor Michael Bloomberg, a billionaire entrepreneur whom many saw as a potential candidate for president, expressed an extreme but frank version of this ideology as it affects immigration when he recently told a Senate committee: "It is as if we expect border control agents to do what a century of communism could not: Defeat the natural forces of supply and demand and defeat the natural human instinct for freedom and opportunity. You might as well sit on the beach and tell the tide not to come in."[35]

Bizarre as is Bloomberg's comparison of the men and women of the U.S. Border Patrol to the wardens of the Soviet empire, his sentiments on supply and demand as "natural forces" that trump and must overwhelm the security and welfare of the American people only echoes the beliefs of numerous important thinkers and activists among Republicans and

35

conservatives. In 2006 a letter published in the *Wall Street Journal* demanded that conservatives either support the "comprehensive" path to amnesty advocated by Ted Kennedy, Hillary Clinton, Barack Obama, Harry Reid, and Nancy Pelosi—as well as by George Bush and John McCain—or lose power and slip into historical oblivion. Quite as important as the letter's hectoring tone were its thirty-three signatories, who include some of the most important policymakers, thinkers, and doers in the conservative Republican movement, including former presidential candidate and media billionaire Steve Forbes, former Congressman and presidential nominee Jack Kemp, former Secretary of State George Shultz, former UN ambassador Jeanne Kirkpatrick, and influential neoconservative editors Bill Kristol and John Podhoretz.[36]

This ideology, which some call "economism," has become increasingly common during the recent economic boom. While it is tempting to represent it as a mere fig leaf for rapacious business interests (which, to be sure, have eagerly employed these ideas as justification), the belief system whereby economic proliferation is not only a good, but the supreme human good, deserves to confronted on its own merits. As Ronald Reagan once noted, "A nation without borders is not really a nation." To be sure hardcore libertarians who reject the state entirely—and thus esteem the American nation less than a lemonade stand. More practical proponents of the idea that America should throw open its borders to virtually all comers have attempted to reconcile the difference between a nation-state and a market place by the claim that the U.S. is and always has been a "proposition nation," i.e., one in which adherence to a set of rules and values suffices for citizenship.[37]

In fact, the rules and values that characterize America have been created and reflect, as well as mold, the traditions and the aspirations of the flesh and blood people who created and sustain the nation. That they continue to lure immigrants of very different creeds and stocks is an argument for the merits of America's population as established, with gradual modification, throughout its history—not evidence, as the "economist" ideologues and their materialist mirrors on the Marxist left would have it, that the foundations of Americanism can be quickly mastered and put in practice, as if they were the rules to Parcheesi or poker. And, of course, one of the most important rules in the American canon—that in the end the people are supreme—gives Americans every right to safeguard their borders and promote their own general welfare, both against enemies encroaching from without and undermining from within.

Endnotes

1. http://www.nytimes.com/2007/06/24/washington/24immig.html?_r=1&pagewanted=2&oref=slogin
2. http://www.ontheissues.org/Celeb/George_W__Bush_Immigration.htm
3. http://ourworld.compuserve.com/homepages/JWCrawford/HCR9.htm
4. http://www.breitbart.com/article.php?id=D8G6U2ko8&show_article=1
5. http://en.wikipedia.org/wiki/Comprehensive_Immigration_Reform_Act_of_2006
6. http://en.wikipedia.org/wiki/Comprehensive_Immigration_Reform_Act_of_2007
7. http://www.whitehouse.gov/news/releases/2006/05/20060515-8.html
8. http://www.ontheissues.org/Celeb/George_W__Bush_Immigration.htm
9. http://www.ontheissues.org/Celeb/George_W__Bush_Immigration.htm
10. http://www.clinton.senate.gov/issues/immigration/index.cfm?topic=march72006
11. http://www.ontheissues.org/2008/Hillary_Clinton_Immigration.htm
    http://profiles.numbersusa.com/improfile.php3?DistSend=NY&VIPID=896#Inviting/Repelling%20Illegal%20Aliens
12. http://www.ontheissues.org/2008/Hillary_Clinton_Immigration.htm
13. http://www.ontheissues.org/2008/Hillary_Clinton_Immigration.htm
14. http://www.barackobama.com/issues/pdf/ImmigrationFactSheet.pdf

15. http://www.barackobama.com/issues/pdf/
ImmigrationFactSheet.pdf
http://thomas.loc.gov/cgi-bin/query/D?c110:3:./
temp/~c110zVcJlA::
16. http://www.ontheissues.org/International/Barack_Obama_
Immigration.htm
17. http://en.wikipedia.org/wiki/Secure_America_and_Orderly_
Immigration_Act_%28S._1033%29
http://www.google.com/search?q=Obama+immigration+FAIR
usa&btnG=Search&hl=en
18. http://www.ontheissues.org/2008/John_McCain_Immigration.
htm
19. http://www.ontheissues.org/celeb/John_McCain_
Immigration.htm
20. http://www.ontheissues.org/celeb/John_McCain_
Immigration.htm
http://en.wikipedia.org/wiki/Arizona_Proposition_200_(2004)
21. http://www.usnews.com/articles/news/campaign-
2008/2008/03/17/where-clinton-obama-and-mccain-stand-on-
immigration.html
http://www.ontheissues.org/celeb/John_McCain_
Immigration.htm
22. http://www.ontheissues.org/celeb/John_McCain_
Immigration.htm
23. http://www.numbersusa.com/PDFs/Reid-comp%20
immig%20reform%20_S.%201348%20CM_.pdf
24. http://www.numbersusa.com/interests/legislation_
proposed110.html
http://profiles.numbersusa.com/improfile.
php3?DistSend=NV&VIPID=556
25. http://profiles.numbersusa.com/improfile.
php3?DistSend=IL&VIPID=255
26. http://www.ontheissues.org/CA/Nancy_Pelosi_Immigration.
htm
http://profiles.numbersusa.com/improfile.
php3?DistSend=CA&VIPID=61
http://www.ontheissues.org/CA/Nancy_Pelosi_Immigration.
htm
27. http://profiles.numbersusa.com/improfile.
php3?DistSend=KY&VIPID=328
http://www.ontheissues.org/Senate/Mitch_McConnell.htm
28. http://www.ontheissues.org/International/Jon_Kyl_

Immigration.htm
http://profiles.numbersusa.com/improfile.
php3?DistSend=AZ&VIPID=35
29. http://www.ontheissues.org/Senate/Trent_Lott.htm
30. http://profiles.numbersusa.com/improfile.
php3?DistSend=ID&VIPID=248
31. http://www.signonsandiego.com/news/politics/
recall/20031010-9999_1n10license.html
32. http://www.pbs.org/newshour/updates/north_america/july-
dec07/spitzer_11-14.html
33. http://www.nytimes.com/2006/05/17/us/17govs.html?_r=1&
pagewanted=2&fta=y&oref=slogin
http://en.wikipedia.org/wiki/Janet_Napolitano
34. http://en.wikipedia.org/wiki/Sanctuary_city
http://www.frontpagemag.com/Articles/Read.
aspx?GUID=C6F068B7-39EA-48CA-8ED2-B03BB095DF44
35. http://www.ontheissues.org/2008/Mike_Bloomberg_
Immigration.htm
36. http://www.opinionjournal.com/extra/?id=110008631
37. http://en.wikipedia.org/wiki/Libertarian_perspectives_on_
immigration

3

THE LEGAL ARENA

◈◈

T HE EVENTUAL DEFEAT OF California's Proposition 187, a 1994 voter-approved initiative endorsed by former California Governor Pete Wilson (approved by 58.8 percent of California voters), which would have denied state benefits (social services, health care, and public education) to illegal aliens and therefore removed the incentives of state-sponsored services and benefits that continue to draw large numbers of illegal aliens to the state, illustrates how the legal system has been used by mass immigration advocates to halt policy prohibitions against illegal immigration. Prop. 187 worked its way through the courts after a federal judge issued a temporary restraining order halting its full implementation two days after becoming state law. California Governor Gray Davis "dropped the appeals process before the courts, effectively killing the law"[1] early in his tenure as governor.

The U.S. legal arena is one area where open-border activists have successfully advanced their mass-immigration agenda. By taking advantage of a tangled web of immigration and asylum laws, open-border activists have pursued their agenda in the U.S. courts and effectively blocked voter-approved initiatives that would impose tougher sanctions against illegal aliens. Liberal judges, in rendering legal decisions to reverse voter-approved initiatives or local ordinances, whether issuing driver's licenses or providing taxpayer-funded financial assistance for out-of-state tuition costs to illegal aliens, have imposed their own interpretations in case after case that make it increasingly difficult for state and local governments to stem the tide of illegal immigration and seal off America's southern border. The burden is increasingly placed on federal-elected officials to take up the matter in Congress since state and local policies are sometimes rendered unconstitutional by the courts. Time and again the roadblocks to effective immigration enforcement has been the usual catch-all legal impediments: violations of "due process" or "equal protection" (as the courts have interpreted the 14th Amendment) and jurisdictional overreach (enforcement measures as exclusively a federal matter).

To give the reader some idea of the extensive reach and convoluted structure of the U.S. legal system governing immigration law, consider the various legal resources available from Cornell University's Law Library as the tip of the iceberg on immigration law. The Cornell Law Library provides researchers with numerous sources across five major categories: (I) Important Secondary Sources, (II) Administrative Decisions, (III) Web Sites, (IV) Federal Resources, and (V) Law Review Articles. Below are examples of the extensive body of immigration law:

Immigration Law and Procedure, 20 volumes;
Stephen Yale-Loehr, co-author;
analysis of law, text of statutes and regulations, procedural manuals
KF 4815 .G66

Interpreter Releases: Report and Analysis of Immigration & Nationality Law
synthesis of current topics and digest of recent decisions with analysis
published weekly
KF 4815 .A51
Microfilm 125, 1921-1971

Immigration Briefings

monthly publication on one major immigration topic
KF 4802 .I334
Westlaw: IMMIGRBRIEF database, 1988-

Bender's Immigration Bulletin, current awareness service includes articles,
federal cases, BIA decisions, final, interim, & proposed rules and regulations.
KF 4221 .A65452

Kurzban's Immigration Law Sourcebook: A Comprehensive Outline and Reference Tool
KF4819.3 .K96 on Reference

Administrative Decisions under Immigration and Nationality Laws,
1940/43 - 1989/95 official reporter of precedential "interim decisions" of the Board of Immigration Appeals, cite as I&N Dec., 1962 -
KF 4812 .A23;

Interim Decisions Service, KF 4812 .A24
Lexis: Immigration > Administrative Materials & Regulations > Agency Decisions > Immigration Precedent Decisions, 1940 -
Westlaw: FIM-BIA database, 1940 –

Hein's Cumulative Index to Interim Precedent Decisions of the Board of Immigration Appeals, 1940-1995
best index to the official reporter above
KF 4812 .7 .H47

Administrative Decisions Under Employer Sanctions & Unfair Immigration-Related Employment Practices Law, Office of the Chief Administrative Hearing Officer, 1988 -
KF 4182 .A2 U58

Lexis: Immigration > Administrative Materials & Regulations > Agency Decisions >
Office of Chief Admin. Hearing Officer Immigration Review Decisions, 1988 -
Westlaw: FIM-OCAHO, 1988 -

Administrative Appeals Unit Decisions
Lexis: Immigration > Administrative Materials & Regulations >
Agency Decisions >

Board of Immigration Appeals (BIA) & AAU Non-Precedent
Decisions
Westlaw: FIM-AAU, 1989-

Board of Alien Labor Certification Appeals Decisions
Lexis: Immigration > Administrative Materials & Regulations >
Agency Decisions >

Board of Alien Labor Certification Appeals Decisions, May 1987-
Westlaw: FIM-BALCA database, November 20, 1987 -

INS General Counsel Opinions
Lexis: Immigration > Administrative Materials & Regulations >
Agency Decisions > INS and DOJ Legal Opinions
Westlaw: FIM-GCO

Law schools throughout the country are offering specialized courses and programs in immigration law. Here's how the School of Professional Studies at CUNY lists their programs and courses for immigration law:

> With forty percent of New Yorkers born in other countries, professionals in many different fields are faced with their employment and family issues on a regular basis. A growing number of paralegals, social workers, lawyers, community advocates, and government officials are turning to SPS to learn about the complex and ever-changing field of immigration law and regulation from practicing lawyers and judges.

> These innovative courses offer a unique opportunity for those working with immigrants and their employers and families to:

> ◄ Understand law and regulations governing immigration and citizenship

> ◄ Learn how to comply with rapidly evolving immigration laws

◄   Learn how to file petitions and applications

◄   Witness immigration court proceedings first hand

◄   Work with top CUNY faculty and legal experts

◄   Gain expertise to advanced professionally

NATIONAL IMMIGRATION FORUM (NIF)

Established in 1982, the National Immigration Forum bills itself as "the nation's premier immigrant rights organization." Authors William Hawkins and Erin Anderson note:

> The NIF was founded in 1982 by Dale Frederick "Rick" Swartz, who had directed the immigrant rights project at the Lawyers Committee for Civil Rights and who had worked closely with the National Lawyers' Guild. Harriet Schaffer Rabb, Ford Foundation Trustee and Co-Director of the Immigration Law Clinic at Columbia School of Law, played a major role in helping Swartz found the new group. Swartz continued his work to secure asylum for Haitian and Central American refugees, to legalize the status of millions of other immigrants and to battle the English Only movement, which seeks to make English the official language of the United States.[2]

The National Immigration Forum has spearheaded a coalition of some 250 national organizations and thousands of local groups. The NIF opposes the Clear Law Enforcement for Criminal Alien Removal (CLEAR) Act of 2007, H.R. 842, which proposed to extend enforcement of federal immigration laws to state and local authorities. The CLEAR Act also provides tougher penalties for aliens in violation of federal immigration law.

In the past, the NIF has received grants from the John D. and Catherine T. MacArthur Foundation. Over a four-year span, 2002-2005, the NIF has received $8,614,320 in total grants and donations.

According to the NIF website,

The Forum is dedicated to embracing and upholding America's tradition as a nation of immigrants. The Forum advocates and builds public support for public policies that welcome immigrants and refugees and are fair to and supportive of newcomers to our country.

We are unique in that we do not have a specific constituency — we speak for immigration in the national interest. The Forum serves as the lead convener of hundreds of associate organizations and other national groups on a range of immigration policy issues, and has been the driving force behind many immigration policy victories. The Forum also works closely with local advocates and service providers across the country.

NIF explains that "[d]uring the past twenty years, the Forum's program efforts have had a direct effect on immigration policies. The Forum strives to influence views in the field, on Capitol Hill and with the general public. Our activities include:

◄ *Building alliances and a stronger field:* In support of the organization's policy objectives, the Forum builds nimble alliances with stakeholders from across the country and across the political spectrum, and supports a growing network of service providers and advocates with updates, strategy recommendations, and meetings and conferences.

◄ *Engaging in direct advocacy:* Within the limits of relevant legal and funding restrictions, the Forum works closely with elected and appointed policy makers at the federal, state, and local level to press for fair and generous immigration-related policies.

◄ *Conducting effective media and public outreach:* The Forum is a reliable and trusted resource for print and electronic journalists, keeping reporters up-to-date with timely information, providing comment on trends and policies, and making referrals to other spokespeople and experts. The Forum provides the public with accessible information through its website and publishes studies and backgrounders that are widely disseminated. The Forum also shares its communications expertise through regular trainings and seminars for immigrant leaders and advocates and Forum staff members are frequently asked to make presentations to diverse audiences throughout the country."

The NIF officers and board of directors include a number of business executives, directors of public interest groups, the U.S. Conference of Catholic Bishops, the Hebrew Immigrant Aid Society, American Nursery and Landscape Association, and the U.S. Chamber of Commerce:

Officers

John Gay, Chair
National Restaurant Association

Ali Noorani, Vice Chair
Massachusetts Immigrant and Refugee Advocacy Coalition

Jeanne Butterfield, Secretary
American Immigration Lawyers Association

Directors

Julie Anbender
Glover Park Group

Kevin Appleby
United States Conference of Catholic Bishops

Gideon Aronoff
Hebrew Immigrant Aid Society

Andrea Bazan-Manson
Triangle Community Foundation

Linton Joaquin
National Immigration Law Center

Randel Johnson
U.S. Chamber of Commerce

Eun Sook Lee
National Korean American Service & Education
Consortium

David Lubell
Tennessee Immigrant and Refugee Rights Coalition

Margie McHugh
Migration Policy Institute

Christopher Nugent
Holland and Knight

Ramon Ramirez
Piñeros y Campesinos Unidos del Noroeste (PCUN)

Craig Regelbrugge
American Nursery & Landscape Association

Angelica Salas
Coalition for Humane Immigrant Rights of Los
Angeles

Helen Samhan
Arab American Institute Foundation

Lisa Versaci
Democracy Alliance

Paul Virtue
Hogan & Hartson, LLP

AMERICAN IMMIGRATION LAWYERS ASSOCIATION (AILA)

One organization at the forefront of the legal trenches in liberalizing America's immigration laws and providing information, professional services, support and educational counseling to litigators as a nonprofit organization is the American Immigration Lawyers Association (AILA). AILA, which consists of some 8,000 lawyers and law professors, listed $9,868,162 in total revenue for its 2005 budget. AILA has established a "Workplace Raids Action Plan" as part of the AILA "Workplace Enforcement Response" to respond to the Immigration and Customs Enforcement (ICE) crackdown on employers who hire illegal aliens. The AILA offers a checklist of procedures for local affiliates of "what-to-do-if" scenarios that should be handled within the first 24 hours of an ICE raid.

AMERICAN CIVIL LIBERTIES UNION (ACLU)

The American Civil Liberties Union (ACLU) remains one of the more aggressive legal organizations working to promote mass-immigration. Claiming to represent "immigrants' rights," the ACLU is "one of the nation's leading advocates for the rights of immigrants, refugees and non-citizens, challenging unconstitutional laws and practices, countering the myths upon which many of these laws are based." The ACLU has launched the "Immigrants' Rights Project" and applauded the federal court decisions striking down anti-immigrant ordinances in Hazelton, Pennsylvania, and Riverside, New Jersey.

In conclusion, a vast network of legal organizations including the National Lawyers Guild (with some 8,000 members and 83 lawyers' chapters nationwide), MALDEF, and the organizations listed above are actively working to advance radical immigration measures and to dismantle policies that restrict the flow of immigration from the Third World.

Endnotes

1. http://en.wikipedia.org/wiki/California_ Proposition_187_(1994)
2. William Hawkins and Erin Anderson, *The Open Borders Lobby and the Nation's Security After 9/11* (Los Angeles, CA: Center for the Study of Popular Culture, 2004): 33.

4

THE CORPORATE FIELD
AND ORGANIZED LABOR

❧

As regards immigration policies, the less said the
better. It may be hoped that world prosperity, increased
political security, and ultimate leveling of birth rates may
diminish migration pressures. Wholly free migration,
however, is neither attainable politically or desirable.
To insist that a free-trade program is logically or
practically incomplete without free migration is either
disingenuous or stupid. Free trade may and should raise
living standards everywhere (and more if transportation
were costless). Free migration would level standards,
perhaps without raising them anywhere (especially
if transportation were costless)—not to mention the
sociological and political problems of assimilation.

—Henry Simons
Economic Policy for a Free Society

MORE THAN EIGHTY YEARS AFTER President Calvin Coolidge
declared, "The business of America is business," millions
of Americans continue to regard business and business
interests as not only pro-American, but as the quintessence of
Americanism. Yet for the past several decades, big business
in America has played a leading role in the drive for open
borders and uncontrolled immigration.

51

To be sure, industrialists have long lobbied for their particular economic interests, including the import of cheap foreign labor. The propaganda in favor of uncontrolled immigration from today's business leaders echoes the arguments California business magnates made in support of bringing in hundreds of thousands of Chinese coolies to work on the railroads and in agriculture in the 1880s. Yet there is an important difference. Until recently, advocates for American business took care to claim that their demands served the interests of the nation and its people. Today, a growing and significant segment of America's most important business interests is not only striving for, but openly espouses, the opening of America's borders and the eclipse of its national sovereignty.

BUSINESS BEFORE BORDERS

Although widely perceived as a disinterested civic group, the U.S. Chamber of Commerce (USCC) has been since its inception nearly a century ago the world's largest business federation and the leading lobbyist, propagandist, and legal bulwark for profit-making companies in America. The USCC defines its core mission as "to fight for business and free enterprise before Congress, the White House, regulatory agencies, the courts, the court of public opinion, and governments around the world."[1]

The Chamber of Commerce has testified frequently before Congress on behalf of amnesty and open-borders legislation, including a "guest worker" and "path to citizenship" program (read: amnesty), expansion of visa programs for foreign workers, and efforts to weaken border security.[2] Four days before the 9/11 attacks were carried out by terrorists able to reside in America due to lax immigration policies, USCC President Thomas Donahue told the Senate Judiciary Committee that immigrants are "our best hope to curb chronic American labor shortages."[3] More recently, the Chamber sent Mitchell Laird, president of MCL Enterprises, Inc., which owns twenty-four Burger King restaurants in Arizona, to lobby a House subcommittee on Social Security for the overturn of Arizona's law against knowingly hiring illegal aliens.[4]

The activities of its lobbyists and lawyers have enabled the Chamber of Commerce to boast that in 2007 it caused the reversal of a decision by the Department of State and the Department of Homeland Security not to accept employer-sponsored permanent visas for foreign workers; to make progress in removing legal provisions that required federal contractors use a government program that would identify illegal employees; to successfully challenge a Department of Homeland Security program that requires the dismissal of employees with faked Social Security numbers; and to organize a nationwide litigation campaign against state and local attempts to take steps against the growing problem of uncontrolled immigration.[5]

Less visible to the public than the Chamber of Commerce's corporate executives, but if anything more persistent and effective in dismantling America's border security, is the USCC's National Chamber Litigation Center (NCLC), which has participated in numerous cases in support of open-borders interests as a party or an amicus curiae. Lawyers from the NCLC were instrumental in reversing the Department of Homeland Security's "No Match" program, which required the dismissal of employees with faked Social Security numbers, in a federal court in 2007. In the same year, NCLC lawyers sued to overturn Arizona's law, opposed by the USCC before Congress, that prevents the knowing employment of illegal aliens. While a federal court dismissed that suit without prejudice, the Chamber's legal arm had more success when, as part of a battery of imported legal firepower, it was able to overturn the efforts of tiny Hazleton, Pennsylvania, to control a flood of illegal aliens through an ordinance banning their hire. The ordinance was overturned by a Pennsylvania district court.[6]

The United States Chamber of Commerce likes to point out that it was founded in response to a call from President William Howard Taft in 1911. But, in fact, the group that President Taft desired was to "keep purely American interests in a closer touch with different phases of commercial affairs"—a far cry from the present policies of the Chamber.[7]

EMPLOYERS TO THE WORLD

Almost as influential as the U.S. Chamber of Commerce, and no less devoted to open borders, is an organization known as the Business Roundtable. An association of the CEOs of American companies with a combined $4.5 trillion in annual revenues and over ten million employees, the Business Roundtable marshals the talents and energies of the executive elite it comprises to "recommend policy and lobby Congress and the Administration on select issues."[8]

Business Roundtable Chairman Harry McGraw, president and CEO of McGraw-Hill, has spoken out forcefully and frequently on immigration. Following the defeat of President Bush's 2007 amnesty bill in the Senate, McGraw called the bill's defeat "deeply disappointing" and the "status quo [i.e., such immigration controls as remain] unacceptable."[9]

Unlike the Chamber of Commerce, which battles to protect unskilled illegal employees from detection, the Business Roundtable focuses on importing skilled foreign workers.

In 2006 McGraw called for a four-fold increase in H-B1 visas for such employees, whom corporations often use to replace Americans, at reduced compensation.[10] The Business Roundtable deploys "task forces," headed by member CEOs, to research and report on issues of interest to the 160 CEOs. One aim of its Task Force on Education and the Workforce is to push for policies that "attract and retain highly educated foreign talent,"[11] while its Task Force on International Trade and Investment promotes the alleged benefits of "growing the economy" through outsourcing, the export of American jobs overseas.[12]

Numerous smaller or more specialized business associations are working no less intensely to increase legal immigration and to protect illegal immigration. The National Association of Manufacturers calls "reform" of American immigration law "essential" — so that businesses can bring in vast numbers of permanent and "temporary" workers.[13]

Business lobbies as diverse as the American Health Care Association and the Association of American Florists have called for amnesty for illegals. From information technology to apple picking, American business leaders have decided that foreign workers are better trained, cheaper, or more easily managed than Americans, and they are lobbying to reap the enhanced profits they believe such workers will bring — regardless of the security and the welfare of the American people.[14]

CASES IN POINT

The Arkansas-based Tyson Foods corporation is a representative example of the abuses that occur in order to obtain cheap labor from abroad. Two legal cases in which Tyson, the world's largest processor of chicken, beef, and pork,[15] prevailed nonetheless throw a lurid light on its practices in favoring foreign workers over American ones. In 2001, Tyson Foods was accused by federal prosecutors of conspiring to hire thousands of illegal immigrants from Mexico and Central America. Tyson's lawyers were able to convince a jury that its executives had been unaware of its managers' receiving new hires direct from immigrant smugglers, but few doubted the higher management's complicity.[16]

Tyson's legal problems over illegals did not go away, however. In 2006, a group of Tyson employees filed a class action suit alleging that the company's policy of hiring illegal aliens depressed wages by as much as 30 percent. The plaintiffs also charged that Tyson Foods was conspiring with two Latino pressure groups, the National Council of La Raza and the League of United Latin American Citizens, to favor employment applications bearing Hispanic surnames. Again, the company was able to prevail, chiefly due to judicial tolerance of its laxity in identifying illegal aliens, but the evidence presented in both cases leaves no doubt of the corporation's preference for cheap imported labor over American workers.[17]

Like Tyson's Foods, retail behemoth Wal-Mart, the world's largest corporation, has relied heavily on cheap imported labor.[18] Raids by U.S. immigration authorities in 1998, 2001, 2003, and 2005 uncovered hundreds of illegal workers. Federal investigators revealed that the unlawful immigrant labor, technically hired by independent contractors, was employed with the full knowledge of Wal-Mart executives.[19]

Despite its repeated offenses, Wal-Mart was able to settle the government's 2005 investigation for $11 million, a tiny fraction of the $285 billion in sales it registered the previous year, with no admission of guilt.[20]

That Wal-Mart and Tyson Foods have so far been able to escape major damages from the lawsuits and prosecutions described above is doubtless not a coincidence. According to a 2006 article in *Business Week*, Wal-Mart has become "the number 1 corporate political contributor" at the federal level.[21] Tyson Foods has funneled large contributions to members of the Senate and House agriculture committees; the Tyson family made generous donations to Mike Huckabee, an immigration-friendly Republican candidate for president in 2008; and in 1997, the company paid $6 million in fines for giving a former secretary of agriculture, Mike Espy, "illegal gifts" valued at $12,000.[22]

ORGANIZED LABOR

As we have seen, certain sectors of the business community—service industry, agriculture, and the meat-packing industry among others—continue to rely on access to cheap labor. In addition to the business sphere, organized labor has taken up the cause of mass immigration. The labor movement's position on immigration has shifted over the years. Under the leadership of Samuel Gompers, the American Federation of Labor consistently supported restrictive immigration policies. The AFL pushed for English literacy tests and argued that lax immigration policies proved detrimental to American workers.

In her book *The Mexican Outsiders: A Community History of Marginalization and Discrimination in California*, author Martha Menchaca points out

> At the time, however, Mexican farm workers were excluded from joining the American Federation of Labor (AFL) or any other national labor union (Reisler 1976; Sosnick 1978; Weber 1973). Union leaders shared popular Anglo American stereotypes of Mexicans and were antagonistic toward

them. They believed that Mexican immigrants competed for scarce jobs and that their presence adversely affected American labor. National labor unions were more interested in lobbying against Mexican immigration to the United States than in helping Mexicans organize local unions. For example, the AFL was actively involved in increasing restrictive immigration policies in order to limit the size of the Mexican population in the United States. Its purpose was to protect the American labor market from Mexican immigrants who allegedly depressed wages and lowered employment standards.[23]

Cornell University economist Vernon Briggs, Jr., who has written extensively and has testified before congress about the impact of immigration on America's labor force, explains the changing position of organized labor on the immigration issue:

> Nonetheless, a choice must be made. At every juncture and with no exception prior to the late 1980s, the labor movement either directly instigated or strongly supported every legislative initiative enacted by Congress to restrict immigration and to enforce its policy provisions. Labor leaders intuitively sensed that union membership levels were inversely related to prevailing trends in immigration levels. When the percentage of the population who were foreign born increased, the percentage of the labor force who belonged to unions tended to fall; conversely when the percentage of the population who were foreign born declined, the percentage of the labor force who belonged to unions tended to rise. History has validated those perceptions. To this end, the policy pursuits of the labor movement over these many years were congruent with the economic interests of American workers in general—whether or not they were union members (and most were not).

But by the early 1990s, some in the leadership ranks of organized labor began to waffle on the issue. This was despite the fact that the nation was in the midst of the largest wave of mass immigration in its history while the percentage of the labor force who belonged to unions was plummeting. In February 2000 the Executive Council of the American Federation of Labor – Congress of Industrial Organizations (AFL-CIO) announced it was changing its historic position. It would now support expanded immigration, lenient enforcement of immigration laws and the legislative agenda of immigrant advocacy groups. Subsequently, AFL-CIO officials publicly explained that the organization was now "championing immigrant rights as a strategic move to make immigrants more enthusiastic about joining unions."

In mid-2005, four unions who had belonged to the AFL-CIO disaffiliated and formed a new federation—Change-to-Win (CTW). The largest of these to disaffiliate was the Service Employees International Union (SEIU). While there were other issues involved in this split-up, SEIU had been the leading voice for the efforts to change labor's historic role on the subject of immigration within the AFL-CIO. It continues to be in its new role in CTW.[24]

Briggs points out that the labor movement in the 1880s actually played a role in the passage of the Chinese Exclusion Act, which suspended Chinese immigration for ten years. Organized labor considered the widespread use of Chinese contractors to undercut wages and labor standards for working Americans. Briggs notes that Gompers, in his autobiography, "boasted that 'the labor movement was among the first organizations to urge such policies.' For as he famously stated: 'we immediately realized that immigration is, in its fundamental aspects, a labor problem.'"

58

As America's population expanded and, in the wake of the 1965 Immigration Act and post-1965 "reform" measures and amnesties, as America's population became increasingly "diverse," the interests and ethnic agenda of Hispanic, Asian, and other immigrants increasingly became synonymous with the U.S. national interest and the interests of American workers in general. As immigrants are now considered to be an important constituency of organized labor, organized labor co-opted the agenda of ethnic-immigrant activists in supporting the rights of "indigenous people." In March 2007, the AFL-CIO issued a statement on America's immigration problems, "Unity Blueprint for Immigration Reform," that among other things urged Congress to enact legislation that would permit the free movement of "indigenous people" across borders.[25]

CASA DE MARYLAND

One organization that represents low-income Latino "workers and tenants" is Casa de Maryland. The Casa de Maryland website describes the organization's purpose and history:

> CASA of Maryland was founded in 1985 by representatives of various congregations, both Central Americans and native-born U.S. citizens. CASA was created in response to the human needs of the thousands of Central Americans arriving to the D.C. area after fleeing wars and civil strife in their countries of origin. In the basement of the Takoma Park Presbyterian Church, CASA provided emergency clothing, food, immigration assistance, and English instruction to new immigrant arrivals from Central America. CASA started with a staff of 2, a handful of volunteer teachers, and funds from various congregations.
>
> As the community grew in numbers and its needs grew in complexity, CASA so expanded its programs. In 1991, in response to growing numbers of day laborers congregating on street corners looking for work in the Long Branch neighbor-

hood of Silver Spring, with the support of Montgomery College and private foundations, CASA set up a temporary trailer to provide legal and employment assistance to the workers. In 1993, Montgomery County granted CASA space and funding to operate a formal Center for Employment and Training at 734 University Blvd. East, in Silver Spring. This was CASA's first workers' center, which has served as a model for the creation of numerous other centers in Maryland and across the country.

Today, CASA has programs in employment placement, vocational training, financial literacy, job development, ESL instruction, Spanish literacy, citizenship classes, legal services, health outreach and education, health information services, social services, and community organizing and advocacy. CASA operates 3 workers' centers and a community education center, and is in the process of opening 2 more workers' centers, a vocational training school, and a 20,000 square-foot multicultural center in the heart of Langley Park. Our offices are located throughout the state of Maryland, specifically focusing on our community in Baltimore City, and Prince George's and Montgomery Counties. CASA caters its programs to three main constituencies: low-income women, workers, and tenants .

CASA is currently recognized as the largest Latino and immigrant organization in the state of Maryland, and is the recipient of national and international recognition for its work, including awards such as the Annie E. Casey Foundation's "Families Count!" Award (2005), the National Council of La Raza's "Affiliate of the Year" Award (2004), the Institute for Policy Studies' Letelier-Moffit Domestic Human Rights Award (2003), and the Mexican-American Legal Defense and

Education Fund's Community Service Award (2006). Thanks to partnerships with local governments, private foundations, individuals, congregations, civic associations, and other organizations supporting CASA's work, over 20,000 low-income Latinos and immigrants directly benefit from CASA's programs and services every year.

CASA targets three groups of the low-income Latino and immigrant community:

- Workers
- Women
- Tenants

Overarching goals in working with the Core Constituency are to promote:

- Improved economic conditions
- Improved social conditions
- Structural change that results in concrete improvements in living conditions

CASA achieves these goals through the programmatic work of three departments:

- Education and Leadership Department
- Community Organizing and Political Action Department
- Services, including Health Promotion, Legal/Social Services, and Employment

FY '08 Outcomes for CASA's Targeted Core Constituency: CASA Staff have collaborated with the core constituency to identify the following outcomes for the current fiscal year:

WORKERS

- Decrease in instances of wage theft
- Decrease in barriers to full-time meaningful employment through acquisition of English
- Increased knowledge through financial literacy instruction

61

◄ Effective operation of workers centers
through participatory worker committees

◄ Increased knowledge about employment rights
through technical assistance on legislative and
community lawyering techniques

◄ Improved public health and access to medical care

◄ Increased access to existing services
through referrals

◄ Immigration reform improving
paths to legalization

◄ Legislation enacted in Maryland that
ensures access to drivers' licenses for all

◄ Decrease in visibility of anti-immigrant campaigns

◄ Increase in the number of eligible workers
who naturalize

The fact that mass-immigration, open-borders activists have organized demonstrations on May Day in recent years, which just happens to coincide with the traditional left-wing celebrations of "international workers' day," is not coincidental. The leadership of organized labor and the "immigrant rights movement" are unified in their campaign to demolish America's borders and advance the global Marxist goals of the liberation of oppressed "indigenous peoples."

Endnotes

1. http://www.uschamber.com/about/default.htm
2. http://www.uschamber.com/issues/index/
immigration/default.htm
http://www.uschamber.com/issues/index/
immigration/skilledworkers.htm
3. http://www.washingtonpost.com/wp-dyn/articles/
A64179-2005Mar24.html
4. http://www.uschamber.com/NR/rdonlyres
s2pb3i7rm24xsko7ugd4mwvs7ogesokukacqeloipai6wblfyt
n2ymbc7xtfg/080506laird_eevs.pdf
5. http://www.uschamber.com/issues/accomplishments/
immigration.htm
6. http://www.uschamber.com/nclc/caselist/issues/

immigration.htm

7. http://www.uschamber.com/about/history/default
8. http://www.businessroundtable.org/
9. http://www.allbusiness.com/services/business-services/4546219-1.html
10. http://www.businessroundtable.org/newsroom/document.aspx?qs=5996BF807822B0F1ADC478E22FB5171 1FCF53CE
11. http://www.businessroundtable.org/taskForces/taskforce/index.aspx?qs=14A5BF159F8
12. http://www.businessroundtable.org//taskForces/taskforce/issue.aspx?qs=6585BF159F249514481138A6DBE 7A7A19BB6487B1693E
13. http://www.nam.org/policypositions/
14. http://www.fairus.org/site/PageServer?pagename=iic_ immigrationissuecentersa5ad
15. http://en.wikipedia.org/wiki/Tyson_Foods
16. http://www.cbsnews.com/stories/2003/03/26/national/main546248.shtml
    http://www.cbsnews.com/stories/2003/02/05/national/main539521.shtml
17. http://www.marketwatch.com/news/story/tyson-foods-illegal-hiring-lawsuit/story.
    aspx?guid=%7B624A31DE-832D-4EEA-A6FE-B979EC2C859F%7D
    http://lawprofessors.typepad.com/immigration/files/trollinger20213081.txt
18. http://en.wikipedia.org/wiki/Wal-Mart
    http://en.wikipedia.org/wiki/Criticism_of_Wal-Mart#Use_of_illegal_workers
19. http://www.cbsnews.com/stories/2003/11/04/national/main581731.shtml
20. http://www.marketwatch.com/News/Story/Story.
    aspx?guid=%7B0B2D4368-AB98-4EF5-8050-5038D0DE3BFD%7D&siteid=mktw&dist=
21. http://www.corporations.org/pipermail/corporations_ corporations.org/2004-March/000216.html
22. http://www.arkansasnews.com/archive/2004/10/31/WashingtonDCBureau/307598.html
    http://www.newsmeat.com/campaign_contributions_ to_politicians/donor_list.php?candidate_ id=P80003478&li=T

http://en.wikipedia.org/wiki/Mike_Espy
23. Martha Menchaca, *The Mexican Outsiders: A Community History of Marginalization and Discrimination in California* (Austin, TX: University of Texas Press, 1995): 80.
24. http://www.cis.org/articles/2007/briggstestimony052407.html
25. http://www.aflcio.org/issues/civilrights/immigration/upload/UnityBlueprint.pdf

5

THE RELIGIOUS SPHERE

❧

DURING HIS VISIT TO THE United States in April 2008, Pope Benedict XVI addressed the matter of America's immigration policy. Pope Benedict urged President Bush and the nation's Roman Catholic Bishops and Cardinals to continue to open the U.S. borders to Hispanic immigrants. According to the *Houston Chronicle*, the Pope pleaded during a prayer service at the Basilica of the National Shrine of the Immaculate Conception, "I want to encourage you and your communities to continue to welcome the immigrants who join your ranks today, to share their joys and hopes, to support them in their sorrows and trials and to help them flourish in their new home."[1]

Pope Benedict's plea—that the United States should embrace additional Hispanic immigrants—reflects the Catholic Church's position on immigration. The Church sees itself in the role of the "Good Samaritan"—alleviating the suffering of the needy, downtrodden, refuse of the world. This Christian (Catholic and Protestant alike) outreach of "inclusion" extends assistance as a global crusade to end the plight of the poverty-stricken Third World, including the suffering that persists in war-torn Darfur. This outreach also encourages First World nations to increase their levels of assistance to the Third World and adopt higher levels of Third World immigrants and refugee resettlements. Although this transnational policy of "inclusion" is described as "humane" and "compassionate," it often remains out of step with faithful and charitable Christians who champion aggressive enforcement of immigration laws, value national sovereignty, and prefer a policy that *preserves* their national heritage rather than *transforms* it. For many Christians, the desire to assist the plight of the needy is a reality check matched by the laws of unintended consequences: importing the problems of misery, suffering, despair, destitution, and disease with a greater influx of Third World immigrants to the U.S. The attempt to solve one problem leads to additional problems, or to paraphrase Garrett Hardin, "you can't just do one thing."

According to the Pew Research Center survey "Attitudes Toward Immigration: In the Pulpit and the Pew," "nearly half of the public, for instance, agrees with the statement that the growing number of newcomers threaten traditional American customs and values, compared with 45 percent who say that newcomers strengthen American society."[2] The survey found that a majority of the respondents (white non-Hispanic Protestants and Catholics) consider that "immigrants today...are a burden because they take our jobs, housing and health care."[3] The open-border immigration policy of various Christian denominations remains at odds with the perspectives of much of the laity. Dr. James Russell, author of *Breach of Faith: American Churches and the Immigration Crisis*, documents the position of the Christian churches on U.S. immigration policy.[4] From the early settlers to the present, Christianity has been the dominant religious affiliation for a sizable majority of Americans. As Russell points out, divisions between clergy and laity over immigration policy have surfaced as the clergy have pushed their congregations in a direction that doesn't reflect the concerns and interests of the laity. Given the historically prominent place of religion in American society, Christians seem energized over the problems of illegal immigration and willing to voice their concerns, but also seem complacent in challenging the authority of church leaders and religious figures.

Christian clergy continually seek new converts to their religious beliefs and recruit new members to their churches, parishes, and various religious orders and organizations. Proselytizing to the unconverted is an essential aspect of Christian outreach and missionary work. The quest to liberalize America's immigration laws fits hand-in-glove with what the clergy sees as its mission. However, the issues for many faithful Christians are matters of national importance: the failure to halt the uninterrupted flow of illegal immigration and the long-range national and cultural implications of mass immigration. There simply is no end to the task of alleviating all the world's ills. For many faithful Christians, liberalizing America's immigration laws and rushing to create a borderless world, a planet that knows no national boundaries, is an untenable solution to a problem that defies resolution. The concept of community is implicitly one of distinctions, as Peter Brimelow rightly pointed out in *Alien Nation*.[5] Unrestricted illegal immigration undermines the sense of community, a thriving organic assembly of citizens regulated by common interests.

NATIONAL HISPANIC CHRISTIAN LEADERSHIP CONFERENCE

Perhaps the single largest Christian nonprofit organization representing Hispanic evangelicals is the National Hispanic Christian Leadership Conference (NHCLC), founded in 1995 by the Rev. Samuel Rodriguez. One of the more high profile Hispanic evangelical leaders in the U.S., Rev. Rodriguez has been featured in *Newsweek*, National Public Radio, and other mass media outlets as a leader with a growing Hispanic constituency that can make a difference in deciding the outcome of future U.S. elections. The NHCLC website explains the purpose of the organization:

> The National Hispanic Christian Leadership Conference (NHCLC) is committed to serving the 16 million Hispanic born-again Christians in the United States and Puerto Rico across generational, country of origin, and denominational lines on issues that pertain to the family, immigration, economic mobility, education, political empowerment, social justice, and societal transformation. The NHCLC serves and facilitates a representative voice for a growing number of the 18,000 Hispanic churches and 75 denominations

in addition to faith-based organizations, institutes, networks, congregations, and active laity. Hispanic born-again Christians make up 37 percent of the U.S. Hispanic population and 88 percent of all U.S. Hispanic Protestants, 43 percent of all U.S. Hispanic Mainline Protestants, and 26 percent of all U.S. Hispanic Roman Catholics.

The organization was founded with the purpose of providing a unified voice for the Hispanic Born Again Christians of all denominations in the United States of America. Lead [sic] by many of the top Hispanic Christian pastors, denominational leaders, businessmen and civil servants, the NHCLC is one of the preeminent voices in the Hispanic Church today. It actively partners with a number of organizations like the National Association of Evangelicals, World Relief, World Vision, Promise Keepers, Sojourners, Center for American Progress, Evangelicals for Human Rights, Compassion Values Forum, and many other organizations.

The NHCLC seeks the political engagement and empowerment of Hispanics via spiritual progressive leadership. We define progressive in the non partisan connotation of a transformational and Trans-generational model. The NHCLC exists for the purpose of Leading The Hispanic Church, Leveraging The Hispanic Vision, and Lifting The Hispanic Dream. Such cannot be realized without political and social empowerment. Thus, this organization partners with federal and state governments to empower the Latino community. The Latino Community in America has much to offer the American Experience. As a result of a definitive Christian Model, Hispanics will lead, particularly within the urban areas of our nation, an unprecedented reformation and renewal that will enhance our communities.

On March 1, 2006, NHCLC urged President Bush and members of Congress to pass "Comprehensive Immigration Reform legislation" (in essence, lobbying for another amnesty). The text of the NHCLC letter appears below:

Dear President Bush and Members of Congress:

We are writing to you as non-partisan Hispanic Evangelical leaders and churches who are concerned about the issue of immigration and the current polarization of our society. Accordingly, the lack of passage of Comprehensive Immigration Reform legislation has created a reality where our Borders are yet fully secured and the immigrant families a long with the entire Hispanic American community find ourselves facing racial profiling, discrimination and a hostile ethnically polarized environment not seen since the days prior to the successes of the Civil rights movement.

Cities across America are beginning to pass ordinances that in essence legalize racial profiling and place the Latino community in an unnecessary defensive posture. We urge you to pass comprehensive immigration reform. The current state of immigration in this country is a complex situation; nevertheless, we as Americans have the intellectual wherewithal, the political acumen and the spiritual fortitude to reconcile the principles of law and order with a pathway to citizenship for those that seek to live the American Dream.

The National Hispanic Christian Leadership Conference (NHCLC) which is the **National Hispanic Association of Evangelicals** hereby joins with the National Hispanic Christian Coalition for Comprehensive Immigration Reform and other key Latino Evangelical leaders in a call to our Federal Government to unite our Nation and pass Comprehensive Immigration Reform. As the sister organization of the National Association of

Evangelicals, we serve approximately 14.5 Million Hispanic Americans in issues that pertain to the family, immigration, economic mobility, education, political empowerment, and spiritual/moral enrichment. We are all, the NHCLC and partners, wholeheartedly committed to assist in the threading of the Hispanic American narrative. Our desire is for every Latino in America to become a productive citizen, master both the English and Spanish languages, embrace the core values of the American idea and realize the American Dream.

The Hispanic Church in America calls upon President George W. Bush and members of Congress to finally pass and sign into law legislation that will protect our borders, put an end to all illegal immigration, create a market driven guest worker program and facilitate avenues by which the millions of families already in America that lack the legal status can earn such status in a manner that reflects the Judeo Christian Value system this nation was founded upon. Let us protect our borders, protect all our families and thus, protect the American dream.

Rev. Samuel Rodriguez Jr, President, National Hispanic Christian Leadership Conference
Rev. Mark V. Gonzales, President, Hispanic Coalition for Comprehensive Immigration Reform, Public Policy Liaison, National Hispanic Christian Leadership Conference

Endorsements of National Evangelical Organizations, Churches & Leaders:

Rev. Felix Posos, Superintendent Emeritus, Assemblies of God, NPLAD, Chairman NHCLC
Dr. Albert Reyes, President, Baptist University of The Americas, Texas Baptist Convention

70

Dr. Gilbert Velez, Senior Pastor Mercy Church, Laredo, Texas. VP, Public Policy, National Hispanic Christian Leadership Conference
Dr. Angel Nunez, Senior Vice President, National Hispanic Christian Leadership Conference
Dr. Sergio Navarrette, Assemblies of God Superintendent, California, Nevada
Dr. David Lazo, World Harvest Churches
Dr. David Espinoza, Trinity Church, San Fernando, Ca. Vice Chair, National Hispanic Christian Leadership Conference

THE NEW SANCTUARY MOVEMENT

The New Sanctuary Movement reorganized in May 2007. The original Sanctuary Movement of the 1980s provided shelter to Central American refugees who fled to the United States in the wake of repressive measures by Central American governments.

One of the more celebrated cases of an illegal alien being sheltered in a sanctuary is Elvira Arellano, who was arrested outside of Our Lady Queen of Angels Church in Los Angeles on August 19, 2007, and eventually deported to Mexico. Arellano, a Mexican citizen who entered the U.S. in 1997 and eventually worked as a cleaning lady for O'Hara International Airport, took refuge in a Chicago church, Amor De Dios United Methodist Church with Pastor José S. Landaverde, where she lived with her American-born son, Saul, in an apartment above the Church. A second illegal Mexican immigrant, Flor Crisostomo, 28, has taken up sanctuary in the same Chicago church. Immigration and Customs Enforcement (ICE) agents have issued an arrest warrant for Crisostomo's deportation.

CHRISTIANS FOR COMPREHENSIVE IMMIGRATION REFORM

The aggressive push to liberalize America's immigration laws and to dismantle the U.S. border is an ongoing agenda of Left-wing religious activists. Progressive religious leaders bolster a global, transnational perspective on various issues involving immigration, population, multiculturalism, and refugee resettlement policies. In supporting the migration and relocation of populations, these religious progressives minimize the significance of the nation-state. Progressive Christian clergy promote an open-borders agenda. The writings of Jim Wallis, the editor of *Sojourners* magazine and an ardent Left-wing activist for "social justice" campaigns, offer a good example of this open-borders activism. Wallis, who posts commentary on a blog for Beliefnet.com, puts an anti-nationalist interpretation of *Psalm* 2:1-3:

> Why do the nations conspire,
> and the peoples plot in vain?
> The kings of the earth set themselves,
> and the rulers take counsel together,
> against the Lord and his anointed, saying,
> Let us burst their bonds asunder,
> and cast their cords from us.

Wallis played an instrumental role in the founding of Christians for Comprehensive Immigration Reform.

The details of Wallis' background are posted on the DiscovertheNetwork.org website:

> Founded by Jim Wallis, *Sojourners* is a Washington, D.C.-based Christian evangelical ministry professing a devotion to the pursuit of "social justice." Formed in Chicago in 1971 by religious students enrolled at Trinity Evangelical Divinity School in Deerfield, Illinois, *Sojourners* was originally known as the People's Christian Coalition (PCC). The PCC community relocated to Washington, D.C. in 1975, at which time it adopted its new name. An allusion to Biblical pilgrims, the name "Sojourners" signifies, to the organization's members, commitment to a radical social order. "For us," *Sojourners* declares, "the word 'radical' has always meant 'rooted.' The explosive mix of biblical faith and radical social renewal that ignited *Sojourners* in the beginning will continue to fuel our pilgrimage ... in the years to come."

Sojourners' statement of faith spelled out the organization's key tenets: "Violence and war will not resolve the inevitable conflicts between people and nations"; "We refuse to accept structures and assumptions that normalize poverty and segregate the world by class"; and "We believe that gospel faith transforms our economics, gives us the power to share our bread and resources, welcomes all to the table of God's provision, and provides a vision for social revolution."

As one of its first acts, *Sojourners* formed a commune in the Washington, D.C. neighborhood of Southern Columbia Heights. Members shared their finances, participated in various activist campaigns, and organized events at both the neighborhood and national levels. The themes of these campaigns, echoed monthly in the pages of the group's in-house publication *Sojourners*, centered on attacking U.S. foreign policy, denouncing American "imperialism," and extolling Marxist revolutionary movements in the Third World. Giving voice to *Sojourners'* intense anti-Americanism, Jim Wallis called the U.S. "... the great power, the great seducer, the great captor and destroyer of human life, the great master of humanity and history in its totalitarian claims and designs."

In the 1980s the *Sojourners* community actively embraced "liberation theology," rallying to the cause of communist regimes that had seized power especially in Latin America, with the promise of bringing about the revolutionary restructuring of society. Particularly attractive for the ministry's religious activists was the Communist Sandinista regime that took power in Nicaragua in 1979. Clark Pinnock, a disaffected former member of *Sojourners*, revealed in 1985 that the community's members had been "100 percent in favor of the Nicaraguan revolution."

Opposing the policies of the Reagan administration that aimed to undercut the Sandinista regime, *Sojourners* initiated a program called "Witness For Peace," under whose auspices Americans traveled to Nicaragua and returned with reports of humanitarian disasters wrought by the Reagan-backed anti-Communist guerrilla forces. The *Sojourners* delegates insisted that any efforts to undermine Sandinista power violated the Nicaraguan people's "right to self-determination."

Writing in the November 1983 issue of *Sojourners*, ministry leaders Jim Wallis and Jim Rice drafted what would become the charter of leftist activists committed to the proliferation of Communist revolutions in Central America. Titled "Promise of Resistance," this document called on activists to carry out various acts of civil disobedience in order to obstruct any attempt by the United States to invade Nicaragua. CISPES, the propaganda arm of El Salvador's Marxist guerrilla movement, was invited by *Sojourners* to participate in acts of resistance in the event of American military intervention. Nearly 70,000 activists signed the document, which was sent to Congress, President Reagan, the Defense Department, and the CIA.

Steadfast advocates of the nuclear freeze movement, *Sojourners* members maintained that a U.S. nuclear buildup was "an intolerable evil" irreconcilably at odds with Christian teaching, and that "[t]he Reagan Administration remains the chief obstacle to the first step in stopping the arms race." While assailing the Reagan administration's defense buildup, *Sojourners* activists downplayed the threat posed by the Soviet Union, chastising U.S. policy-makers for their tendency "to assume the very worst about their

Soviet counterparts."

With the end of the Cold War, *Sojourners* turned its attention to causes such as environmentalism. In one 1990 *Sojourners* article, for example, writer Bob Hulteen mounted the argument that environmental activism was a logical outlet for the notions of justice long championed by the ministry. "Justice-seeking work without concern for the earth is naïve and narrow minded," Hulteen explained.

The ministry also reviled welfare reform as a "mean-spirited Republican agenda" characterized by "hatred toward the poor" and mounted a defense of affirmative action.

In the fall 1994 issue of *Sojourners*, writer Martha Orianna Baskin assailed the American trade embargo against Cuba. Similarly, the ministry declared against every American military intervention in the 1990s and, more recently, the military campaigns in Iraq and Afghanistan....

The editors of *Sojourners* magazine currently offer a program called "Preaching the Word." For an annual fee of $44.95, religious leaders who share the ministry's commitment to reading scripture through the lens of leftist politics can receive articles to supplement their sermons. According to *Sojourners* editors, "Preaching the Word" is designed for pastors who preach "with the Bible in one hand and the newspaper in the other."

Sojourners also runs an internship program for "anyone 21 years or older who is single or married without dependents," aiming to cultivate a new supply of evangelical activists. Residing, like *Sojourners* of old, in a shared household, *Sojourners* interns are employed full-time at the ministry (or at its sister organization, Call to Renewal), where they work on an "Overcome Poverty" program to advance economic initiatives through specially organized 'preach-ins' and public demonstrations.

Sojourners is a member organization of the Win Without War and United for Peace and Justice anti-war coalitions. It condemns the Guantanamo Bay detention center, where several hundred terrorist suspects are being held by the U.S. government. Said the *Sojourners* website on June 10, 2005:

"Guantanamo Bay has become not only a symbol of the U.S. government's hypocrisy and dishonesty—or 'disassembling,' as President Bush might put it—around the war on terror. The prison camp has become one of the more egregious examples of the cost of unaccountable power. Human rights groups have long documented the abuse of prisoners at Guantanamo, including desecration of the Quran.... The 540 prisoners at the facility have been held incommunicado, denied access to legal counsel, and, in fact, denied the most basic aspects of legal process.... Guantanamo should be closed. But simply closing the facility—and either moving the detainees to another location or returning them to their country of origin—is not enough. If the United States is to regain any credibility as an advocate of human rights around the world, it must begin to practice what it preaches in Iraq, in Afghanistan, in Guantanamo, and everywhere else. The erosion of respect for human rights by U.S. personnel didn't begin at Abu Ghraib or Guantanamo Bay, and the responsibility for it goes all the way to the top."

Sojourners is supported by the Cawley Family Foundation, Crystal Trust, the Delaware Community Foundation, the Max and Victoria Dreyfus Foundation, the Gannett Foundation, the Gill Foundation, the Laffey-McHugh Foundation, the Longwood Foundation, the MBNA Foundation, the Open Society Institute, the Peninsula Community Foundation, and the Philadelphia Foundation.

According to the *Sojourners* website, sojo.net,
the organizations and individuals that make up **Christians for Comprehensive Immigration Reform** are uniting around a shared set of common moral and theological principles:

◄ All people, regardless of national origin, are made in the "image of God" and deserve to be treated with dignity and respect (*Genesis* 1:26-27, 9:6).

◄ An undeniable biblical responsibility to love and show compassion for the stranger among us (*Deuteronomy* 10:18-19, *Leviticus* 19:33-34, *Matthew* 25:31-46).

◄ Immigrants are our neighbors, both literally and figuratively, and we are to love our neighbors as ourselves and show mercy to neighbors in need (*Leviticus* 19:18, *Mark* 12:31, *Luke* 10:25-37).

Respect for the rule of law, but also an obligation to oppose unjust laws and systems that harm and oppress people made in God's image, especially the vulnerable (*Isaiah* 10:1-4, *Jeremiah* 7:1-7, *Acts* 5:29, *Romans* 13:1-7).

Christians for Comprehensive Immigration Reform seeks legislation that is consistent with biblical principles; legislation that protects U.S. borders while establishing a viable, humane, and realistic immigration system. "We propose that Congress pass comprehensive immigration reform that reflects the American commitment to the three formative pillars of our nation: the rule of law, our faith value system and the pursuit of the American Dream," said Rev. Samuel Rodriguez, President of National Hispanic Christian Leadership Conference, America's largest Hispanic Evangelical organization, serving 10,700 Hispanic evangelical churches with 15 million members.

Christians for Comprehensive Immigration Reform supports comprehensive immigration reform legislation that includes:

◄ Border enforcement and protection initiatives that are consistent with humanitarian values while allowing the authorities to enforce the law and implement American immigration policy;

◄ Reforms in our family-based immigration system that reduce the waiting time for separated families to be safely reunited and maintain the constitutionally guaranteed rights of birthright citizenship and the ability of immigrants to earn naturalization;

◄ An opportunity for all immigrant workers and their families already in the U.S. to come out of the shadows and pursue the option of an earned path towards permanent legal status and citizenship upon satisfaction of specific criteria;

◄ A viable guest worker program that creates legal avenues for workers and their families to enter our country and work in a safe, legal, and orderly manner with their rights and due process fully protected and provides an option for workers to gain permanent status independent of an employer sponsor; and

◄ A framework to examine and ascertain solutions to the root causes of migration, such as economic disparities between sending and receiving nations.

Christians for Comprehensive Immigration Reform's biblical and legislative principles **are included in the coalition's** Joint Statement of Principles, which have been signed by a [group] of coalition Christian organizations, churches, and high profile leaders, including, Dr. Joel C. Hunter,

Sammy Mah, World Relief; Rev. Samuel Rodriguez, National Hispanic Christian Leadership Conference; Ron Sider, Evangelicals for Social Action; Jim Wallis, *Sojourners*; Noel Castellanos, Christian Community Development Association; Tony Campolo, The Evangelical Association for the Promotion of Education; World Evangelical Alliance; We Care America; American Baptist Churches USA, Presbyterian Church (USA); United Methodist Church; Mennonite Church USA; and Church World Service.

THE CATHOLIC CHURCH AND IMMIGRATION POLICY

Some 64.3 million Roman Catholics live in the United States, constituting 23 percent of the U.S. population, according to 2004 figures. The Worldwide Catholic population is 1.045 billion. The Catholic population of the U.S. in 1965 was 46.6 million or 24 percent of the total U.S. population. As one of several large organized religious bodies, the Roman Catholic Church, as indicated by its sizable membership, constitutes a large interest-group constituency.

UNITED STATES CONFERENCE OF CATHOLIC BISHOPS

The United States Conference of Catholic Bishops has been at the forefront of efforts to undermine the enforcement of U.S. immigration laws and to seal-off the flow of illegal immigration along the southern border with Mexico. The U.S. Conference of Catholic Bishops urged President Bush to veto the Secure Fence Act of 2006, which:

◄ Authorizes the construction of hundreds of miles of additional fencing along our Southern border;

◄ Authorizes more vehicle barriers, checkpoints, and lighting to help prevent people from entering our country illegally; and

◄ Authorizes the Department of Homeland Security to increase the use of advanced technology like cameras, satellites, and unmanned aerial vehicles to reinforce our infrastructure at the border.

The letter of the U.S. Conference of Catholic Bishops, dated October 10, 2006, opposed the legislation because "we believe it could lead to the deaths of migrants attempting to enter the United States and increased smuggling-related violence along our border. We also believe it would send the wrong signal to our peaceful neighbor to the south, Mexico, as well as the international community. Finally, we do not believe it will solve the problem of illegal immigration faced by our nation."

CATHOLIC LEGAL IMMIGRATION NETWORK (CLINIC)

Another Catholic organization that promotes an open-borders agenda is the Catholic Legal Immigration Network (CLINIC). According to information on the CLINIC website:

The Catholic Legal Immigration Network, Inc. takes its inspiration and shape from Catholic social teaching, particularly Church teaching on migrants and newcomers.

In January 2003, the U.S. and Mexican bishops released an historic pastoral statement on migration titled "Strangers No Longer: Together on the Journey of Hope." This document builds on a rich tradition of Catholic social thought and forms the basis of the Church's "Justice for Immigrants" campaign.

PROTESTANT DENOMINATIONS

LUTHERAN CHURCH—MISSOURI SYNOD

The Lutheran Church has encouraged the resettlement of refugees and "caring for immigrants" as noted in a Church statement posted on the Lutheran Church—Missouri Synod (LCMS) website:

Recent LCMS conventions have adopted several resolutions encouraging ministry to immigrants and refugees.

At the 2004 convention, resolution 6-01 reiterated the priorities for human care, which included "caring for immigrants and refugees." Resolution 6-06 expanded on this priority:

To Support
Refugee/Immigrant/Asylee Resettlement
RESOLUTION 6-06

WHEREAS, Holy Scripture directs Christians to show love, care, hospitality, and assistance toward the strangers and foreigners in our lands; and

WHEREAS, Millions of refugees are in desperate need of our Christian charity and support; and

WHEREAS, Lutheran Immigration and Refugee Service (LIRS) is the second largest agency currently providing for the orderly admission of refugees to the United States (as regulated by Congress); and

WHEREAS, The ministries of LIRS offer congregations opportunities to provide Christian charity and support; therefore be it

Resolved, That we encourage our congregations, Districts, synodical church officials, boards, and agencies to petition our federal and state governments and their agencies to continue funding existing refugee or immigrant or asylee resettlement programs and agencies; and be it further

Resolved, That we encourage our congregations, individually or jointly, to contact LIRS, LCMS World Relief, and/or local Lutheran social agencies or services for information and assistance to resettle at least one refugee or immigrant or asylee family as soon as possible and that this action be taken to carry out the Great Commission.

Action: Adopted [Yes: 1078; No: 52]

The convention also adopted resolution 1-07, emphasizing ethnic and urban ministry, including work among immigrant groups. The resolution encouraged congregations, circuits, and mission partnerships "to identify their opportunities for mission among people of other cultures, races, and generations and to seek strategies for appropriate missional approaches with these groups, with support of the District staff."

Similarly, the 2001 convention adopted resolution 6-11, "To Support Refugee Resettlement." The 1998 convention adopted resolution 1-03A, "To Encourage All Congregations and Districts to Support Multicultural Mission Efforts."

And in 1995, the convention adopted resolution 1-04A, "To Further Evangelistic Outreach among Immigrants," in which "The Lutheran Church — Missouri Synod reaffirm[ed] its conviction that it is the will of the Lord that His people reach out with love and faith to the immigrants that He has placed in their midst and seek ways to serve them in their time of need (Lev. 19:33-34)."[6]

CHURCH WORLD SERVICE (CWS)

Founded in 1946, Church World Service (CWS) is a cooperative of 35 Protestant, Orthodox, and Anglican denominations that provides assistance to refugees and uprooted asylum seekers. CWS explains its mission and purpose:

Nearly 35 million people around the world are uprooted from their homes and communities by persecution and armed conflict. The Immigration and Refugee Program of Church World Service (CWS/IRP) is an ecumenical family empowering churches to show hospitality to strangers, that is, to immigrants, refugees, asylum seekers and other uprooted people in the United States and around the world. CWS/IRP resettles about 8,000 refugees and entrants in the United States each year, and also helps meet the needs of people in protracted refugee situations and refugees returning home.

It should be noted that many other mainline Protestant denominations, including the United Church of Christ, United Methodist Church, and the ecumenical National Council of Churches, have historically supported the sanctuary movement, fostered the development of refugee resettlement assistance, and promoted unrestricted immigration.

JEWISH ORGANIZATIONS

Some of the more enthusiastic supporters of open-borders, mass immigration have come from Jewish organizations. Symbolic of this support is the famous sonnet, "The New Colossus," of Emma Lazarus (1849-1887) engraved on a bronze plaque in the interior of the pedestal at the Statue of Liberty.[7]

Lazarus, a Jewish-American poet born in New York City, wrote about Jewish themes and served as a passionate advocate for Jewish causes. Lazarus was motivated, in part, by her concern for displaced Jewish refugees, particularly Russian Jews expelled during the pogroms in Czarist Russia of the 1880s. A news feature by Jacki Lyden on NPR's *All Things Considered*, highlighting a new biography of Lazarus, described her as "a Sephardic Jew, a descendant of people expelled from Spain centuries before. She often wrote about the 'Jewish plight' in her poetry. She was an early Jewish nationalist— advocating for a Jewish state in Palestine as early as the 1880s. [N]ear the end of her life she became an advocate for disenfranchised immigrants, who were arriving by the thousands in the late 1800s."[8]

Open-border advocates often invoke Lazarus's sonnet to advance their political agenda. The sonnet, reprinted on page 84, illustrates the mindset of enthusiasts of unrestricted immigration, particularly among Jewish activists. Lazarus's sentiments serve as a propaganda ploy to counter any policy restrictions on immigration.

The New Colossus
Not like the brazen giant of Greek fame,
With conquering limbs astride from land to land;
Here at our sea-washed, sunset gates shall stand
A mighty woman with a torch, whose flame
Is the imprisoned lightning, and her name
Mother of Exiles. From her beacon-hand
Glows world-wide welcome; her mild eyes command
The air-bridged harbor that twin cities frame.

"Keep, ancient lands, your storied pomp!" cries she
With silent lips. "Give me your tired, your poor,
Your huddled masses yearning to breathe free,
The wretched refuse of your teeming shore.
Send these, the homeless, tempest-tossed to me,
I lift my lamp beside the golden door!"
—**Emma Lazarus, 1883**

Professor Kevin MacDonald has detailed the Jewish involvement in immigration policy from the late 1800s to 1965. In a lengthy paper published in the academic journal *Population and Environment*, MacDonald argues that prominent American Jews took an active role in shaping United States immigration policy.[9] MacDonald points out that Jews have historically opposed the establishment of "ethnically and culturally homogeneous societies in which they reside as minorities." Consequently, Jews took an active role in opposing the 1924 Immigration Act and, in the aftermath of federal restrictions on immigration, led the drive to liberalize America's immigration policies in Congress and other public venues.

The American Jewish Committee highlights the historic role that American Jews have played in welcoming "strangers" to the United States while also emphasizing the need for border security in the wake of the 9/11 terrorist attacks:

> American Jews have consistently maintained a deep interest in United States immigration and refugee policy. According to Jewish tradition,

"strangers" are to be welcomed and valued, as we were once "strangers in the land of Egypt." From its founding in 1906, the American Jewish Committee (AJC) has been a strong voice in support of immigration, participating actively in many of the major immigration debates of our time: opposing reductions in the flow of legal immigrants; supporting increased "family unification" immigration; supporting efforts to reduce the flow of illegal immigration within the context of established civil liberties protections; supporting generous immigration policies regarding refugees who are fleeing persecution, as defined by U.S. law; opposing the denial of government benefits to non-citizen legal immigrants; and supporting programs designed to educate and integrate new citizens.

Today, AJC finds itself faced with the reality of a changed set of circumstances. In the years leading up to the terrorist attacks of September 11, 2001, the borders of the United States were relatively open. The economy was booming and immigration was looked upon favorably. With Mexico's newly elected president, Vicente Fox, the United States was working toward an accord to facilitate immigration between our two nations. But after nineteen radical Islamic terrorists entered the country to carry out the tragic events of September 11, 2001, U.S. immigration policy has come under fire and is now at the forefront of political debate.

Understanding the significance of these events, AJC recently reaffirmed its commitment to fair and generous immigration policies, as fundamentally good for the United States and consistent with Jewish values. At the same time, AJC is committed more than ever to the need to increase the security of our nation's borders and to better

incorporate newcomers into American society
and culture.[10]

In a departure from the conventional Jewish view of
unrestricted immigration, Stephen M. Steinlight, a former
director of national affairs at the American Jewish Committee,
addressed what he described as divisions within the Jewish
community over immigration policy and national security
concerns in the post-9/11 era in a 2004 paper published by the
Center for Immigration Studies.[11] Steinlight noted:

Thus, behind closed doors, Jewish leaders speak
a different language. This is not entirely new
with immigration, but the gulf is now a chasm.
Privately they express grave concern that unregu-
lated immigration will prove ruinous to American Jewry, as it has for French Jewry, and will for
Jews throughout Western Europe. There's particular fear about the impact on Jewish security, as
well as American support for Israel, of the rapid
growth of the Muslim population. At the conclusion of meetings with national leaders, several
told me, "You're 1000 percent right, but I can't go
out and say it yet." While they have yet to find the
civic courage to break with the traditional consen-
sus they can see the Rubicon glinting in the dis-
tance, and many recognize that eventually they
will have to cross it.... I've spoken about immigration with more grassroots Jews than any other
person in America, and I know that change won't
come painlessly. At a meeting at one of New York
City's most prominent synagogues, board members clashed savagely over my remarks, with the
president of the congregation, who called me a
racist, being attacked by a senior board member
as "the kind of Jew that sold out others to the
Nazis." Segments of the leadership remain true
believers in the dying faith of open immigration,
and will not give up without a fight. But that
change is inevitable is clear enough. The ques-

tion, ultimately, is whether it will come too late to make a difference to the future of America and its Jewish community....

Historical consciousness and political acuity notwithstanding, American Jews, like everyone, believe in myths, which die slowly because they represent values and ideals not realities, and the myth of Jewish immigrant experience will atrophy only gradually. Of all the pieces of Americana that American Jews know by heart, among the most-cherished is that verse inscribed on the base of the Statue of Liberty: "Give me your tired, your poor, your huddled masses yearning to breathe free...."

Written by a Jewish schoolgirl poet inspired by the persecution of Jews in Czarist Russia, for more than a century it's expressed a highly romanticized image of immigration, one that became iconic and all-encompassing despite its irrelevance to much it purports to represent. This quote concerns refugees and asylum seekers and has scant application to immigrants per se. If American Jews are to get this issue right, they must disaggregate the two. Jewish immigrant experience more closely parallels that of refugees and asylum seekers than typical immigrants — then or now.[12]

CONCLUSION

Various religious denominations and sects continue to actively undermine rigorous enforcement of U.S. immigration laws and push an open-borders agenda against the interests and desires of large majorities of the laity. Progressive religious leaders continue to work hand-in-glove with radical Marxists who seek the continuing transformation of the United States into a multicultural, multiethnic, borderless conglomerate. Understanding the prominent role of religious organizations and denominations in dismantling America's borders and national sovereignty is vital in any analysis of the open-borders network.

Endnotes

1. http://www.chron.com/disp/story.mpl/life/religion/5707553.html
2. http://pewresearch.org/pubs/20/attitudes-toward-immigration-in-the-pulpit-and-the-pew
3. Ibid
4. James C. Russell, *Breach of Faith: American Churches and the Immigration Crisis*, Raleigh, North Carolina: Representative Government Press, 2004
5. Peter Brimelow, *Alien Nation: Common Sense About America's Immigration Disaster*, New York: Random House, 1995
6. www.lcms.org/pages/internal.asp?NavID=9989
7. http://www.vdare.com/fulford/statue_of_immigration.htm (For a more detailed explanation of the context of the Statute of Liberty see the text of James Fulford's posting on VDARE.COM)
8. http://www.npr.org/templates/story/story.php?storyId=6359435
9. Kevin MacDonald, "Jewish Involvement in Shaping American Immigration Policy, 1881-1965: A Historical Review, *Population and Environment*: 19, 4, March 1998: 295-356.
10. http://www.ajc.org/site/pp.aspx?c=ijITI2PHKoG&b=838517&printmode=1
11. http://www.cis.org/articles/2004/back404.html
12. Ibid

6

THE FOURTH ESTATE

❧

O NE SIGNIFICANT FACET OF the open-borders network is the role of the Fourth Estate. Commonly identified by con- servative media critics as the "media elite," the mass media and telecommunications industry (major newspapers, wire services, news magazines and networks, and cable service providers) encourage mass immigration, "diversity," multi- culturalism, and the ongoing demographic transformation of American society. The coverage of immigration-related issues, especially over the span of the past decade, confirms the me- dia elite's lack of neutrality and objectivity in scrutinizing the open-borders agenda of mass immigration activists.

Since the 1950s, news organizations have established themselves as independent gate-keepers, serving as sanitation filters of public information. Much of what readers read in daily newspapers and viewers view on televised newscasts reflect preexistent contemporary societal and cultural trends. For example, news content is by and large a reflection of trends, fads, and fashions in American society. However, some media critics view the press as initiating these trends, *creating* artificial interests, needs, and desires and *setting* social, cultural, and national trends and standards.

Journalists, reporters, network news anchors, and commentators often dismiss the idea that the press has any leverage or sway over societal and national affairs. However, journalists are not simply passive observers on the national scene. The daily and weekly decisions to go after some stories rather than others, the limited space in which information is distilled for publication, and the way such stories are covered — the cultivation of sources and contacts, what to emphasize and downplay, the choice of words and phrases (descriptive use of "hate group" and "undocumented" workers), and the overall approach in editing — show that the mass media actively set the scope, direction, tone, and spin of news coverage. Living in an era of managed news, whereby information is filtered to the public in a controlled process, much of the contemporary reportage of the media elite has been carefully crafted and presented through the prism of political correctness.

MEDIA BIAS

Our discussion of the Fourth Estate's practices (as a medium of communication) in covering immigration-related issues will examine the standard conservative criticism of the media elite (liberal bias), consider if such a bias extends beyond the liberal-conservative ideological dichotomy, and raise the prospect if such a bias is recognizable in the news coverage on immigration.

Recent studies confirm what an earlier generation of media critics has identified as a prevalent "liberal bias" in the mass media's news coverage. Tim Groseclose, professor of political science at UCLA, and Jeffrey Milyo, an economist and public policy scholar at the University of Missouri, found among major media outlets "a quantifiable and significant bias in that nearly all of them lean to the [L]eft," according to Milyo, the study's co-author. The authors analyzed twenty major media outlets and found that eighteen scored Left of center. Their results were published in the *Quarterly Journal of Economics*. Contrary to the conventional conservative criticism of National Public Radio as the bastion of liberal bias, Groseclose and Milyo discovered that:

> Another somewhat surprising result is our esti-
> mate of *NPR's Morning Edition*. Conservatives
> frequently list NPR as an egregious example of
> a liberal news outlet. However, by our estimate

the outlet hardly differs from the average mainstream news outlet. For instance, its score is approximately equal to those of *Time, Newsweek,* and *U.S. News and World Report,* and its score is slightly *less* than the *Washington Post's.* Further, our estimate places it well to the right of the *New York Times,* and also to the right of the average speech by Joe Lieberman. These differences are statistically significant. We mentioned this finding to Terry Anderson, an academic economist and Executive Director of the Political Economy Research Center, which is among the list of think tanks in our sample. (The average score of legislators citing PERC was 39.9, which places it as a moderate-right think tank, approximately as conservative as RAND is liberal.) Anderson told us, "When *NPR* interviewed us, they were nothing but fair. I think the conventional wisdom has overstated any liberal bias at NPR." Our *NPR* estimate is also consistent with Hamilton's [2004, p. 108] research on audience ideology of news outlets. Hamilton finds that the average *NPR* listener holds approximately the same ideology as the average network news viewer or the average viewer of morning news shows, such as *Today* or *Good Morning America.* Indeed, of the outlets that he examines in this section of his book, by this measure *NPR* is the ninth most liberal out of eighteen.[1]

Other studies, ranging from surveys by *Editor and Publisher* to the University of Connecticut's Department of Public Policy, have also established a leftward tilt of the media elite's news coverage.[2] Earlier works by David H. Weaver and G. Cleveland Wilhoit[3] as well as Lichter, Rothman, and Lichter[4] confirm a Left- to middle-of-the-road political leaning among journalists (in Weaver and Wilhoit) and a distinct liberal bias (in Lichter, Rothman, and Lichter).

The author's own experience, having worked more than

a decade for a major news organization, provided a glimpse of the inner workings of the national press corps. On balance, some conservative media critics over emphasize the charge of "liberal bias" as if this and this alone explained all one needed to know about the management of contemporary news coverage and the media elite (national news organizations, such as *Time, Newsweek, U.S. News*, the *New York Times, Washington Post*, the *Wall Street Journal*, and network news). The notion that there is some conspiratorial cabal of radical Leftists consciously controlling the news reflects a misunderstanding of the internal operations of news organizations, how the news process works, and the adversarial culture of the mass media. Although studies consistently show a liberal bias among the media elite, much of this bias reflects the adversarial culture of the press. To the extent that a liberal bias *influences* the national news coverage of social and cultural issues, the typical reaction on the part of journalists is much like fish unable to see water. Aaron Wildavsky, the late distinguished political scientist, summarized the specific nature of this media bias:

> The national media has a characteristic bias that could be called American egalitarianism. This bias is not recognized by those who hold it, partly because it seems natural to them (as our biases appear natural to us) and partly because it does not fit neatly into the liberal-conservative or Democratic-Republican dichotomies to which all of us are accustomed. The fact that members of the national media are criticized across the usual political spectrum solidifies their view that they are distributing their blows impartially. Because scholars have not tested for American egalitarianism, they do not find it. A well-known research phenomenon—you only find what you look for— may explain why some of us find biases while many studies deny it.[5]

Wildavsky's claim about the mass media exhibiting an "egalitarian bias" also holds true for the mass media's widespread coverage of racial, cultural, and social issues. One example that would test Wildavsky's thesis is the widespread news coverage of the controversial best-seller *The Bell Curve* by Richard Herrnstein and Charles Murray. The press coverage in the wake of the book's release was overwhelmingly critical, often excoriating the author's motivations in writing the book on a personal level, despite some positive reviews in selected media outlets (mainly conservative-oriented publications) and the scientific literature.[6] Again, Wildavsky puts his finger on what more accurately seems to qualify as a "liberal" bias among journalists, namely an egalitarian predisposition:

> Just as individualists believe in equality of opportunity so as to expand the available resources within which some people can do better than others, and hierarchists believe in equality under the law so that people of different status can be judged according to their positions — egalitarians believe in greater equality of condition so as to reduce disparities in power. Accordingly, they want to diminish differences between rich and poor, black and white, women and men, children and parents, Third and First Worlds, and so on. Because authority is a prima facie case of inequality, they reject it.[7]

Wildavsky's theory of an "egalitarian bias" in the national press corps helps to understand the recent news coverage of the immigration issue, which has been fueled by interest-group politics, considering the highly visible public role of ethnic-immigrant activism since 2006. An estimated 3 million Latino immigrants and illegal aliens took to the streets of two dozen cities, including Los Angeles, Boston, Kansas City, Philadelphia, and Washington, D.C. in the spring of 2006 to lobby Congress on the immigration-border security legislation that was pending before Congress.

In *Time's* cover story of April 10, 2006, "Who Gets To Be an American?," several experts were consulted as to their views on immigration reform. Mark Krikorian, executive director of the Center for Immigration Studies, noted that

> The public is already in favor of immigration

enforcement. It's an elite commitment that's lacking. It's the business elite, Big Labor, Big Religion, Big media, Big academia, who are hostile to the very concept of immigration enforcement.

Newsweek also featured immigration on its cover that same week (April 10, 2006) and took a different approach in highlighting the growing intensity of the issue. Arian Campo-Flores, the lead writer of "America's Divide," "tells the story of a Florida family that has gone in one generation from a penniless mother crossing the Rio Grande to six children who have worked hard, bought homes and become legal, but are still connected to illegals who could be deported under the House bill." Mark Whitaker, *Newsweek*'s former editor, quotes Campo-Flores on covering the mass immigration protests, "Seeing the protests reminds me of the backlash to [California] Gov. Pete Wilson's harsh anti-immigrant measures in the 1990s.... That seriously debilitated the state GOP for years; now the national party risks doing the same, after all of Bush's cultivation of Hispanics." What neither feature story mentioned was that the mass Latino demonstrations that took place in late March and early April 2006 (as well as the Great American Boycott on May 1, 2006, referred to in Spanish as *El Gran Paro Estadounidense*) were highly organized by radical left organizations, including "numerous anti-war, left-wing, socialist and communist groups." According to the Wikipedia website entry on the Great American Boycott:

> The boycott was announced on April 10, 2006 in Los Angeles, California by the March 25 Coalition of Catholic groups, immigration advocacy organizations, and labor unions. Hermandad Mexicana, an affiliate of the Mexican American Political Association, the Coalition for Humane Immigrant Rights of Los Angeles (CHIRLA), Amigos de Orange, and local MEChA chapters all promptly joined. It was coordinated nationally by the May Day Movement for Worker & Immigrants Rights. The coalition arose out of protests against H.R. 4437, a legislative proposal that was passed by

the United States House of Representatives on December 16, 2005 by a vote of 239 to 182, only to die in the United States Senate by not being brought to the floor before the 109th Congress ended. This bill would have made residing in the U.S. illegally a felony and imposed stiffer penalties on those who knowingly employ and harbour non-citizens illegally. It also called for the construction of new border security fences along portions of the 2,000-mile United States–Mexico border. The coalition takes its name from the date of the first mass protest against the bill, a day which saw upwards of 500,000 demonstrators on the streets of Los Angeles, as well as hundreds of thousands in other major U.S. cities.

Numerous anti-war, left-wing, socialist and communist groups also endorsed the Boycott. The Act Now to Stop War and End Racism coalition, in particular, provided signs and mobilized supporters to attend demonstrations, and while the American Civil Liberties Union took no official stance, it offered advice and information for protesters on its website. The AFL-CIO also endorsed the protests, saying that the H.R. 4437 "isn't the answer" to immigration issues. The AFL-CIO's executive vice president, Linda Chavez-Thompson, stated: "We believe that there is absolutely no good reason why any immigrant who comes to this country prepared to work, to pay taxes, and to abide by our laws and rules should be relegated to this repressive, second-class guest worker status."[8]

The *Time* and *Newsweek* accounts on immigration left the reader with the mistaken impression that the mass demonstrations that took place in late March 2006, which partly triggered this news cycle by national media outlets, were spontaneous uprisings rather than well-organized and orchestrated events. Also missing from the coverage is any information about the involvement of militant pro-communist organizations in the mass demonstrations for immigrant rights that occurred in late March 2006 and also on May Day, May 1, 2006. The *Workers World*, a publication of the Workers World Party, a political movement "based on the great revolutionary concepts of Marx and Lenin, which learns from the mass movements while helping them grow and develop... [and] works with others to build the broadest mass actions while promoting the struggle for socialism," posted the following on its website:

May 1 'Great American Boycott of 2006'for immigrant rights gathers momentum

The national call for a May 1 "Great American Boycott of 2006: No Shopping, No School, No Work" to demand full rights for immigrant workers and their families is gathering momentum. This call, initiated by the March 25th Coalition Against HR4437—a grassroots coalition that grew out of the Los Angeles action that brought hundreds of thousands of immigrant workers into the streets last month—has likened the May action to the Montgomery, Ala., bus boycott of 1955. Organizers want to exercise both political and economic power on that day.

The call has struck a chord in many immigrant communities. For many immigrant workers May 1 is celebrated in their home countries as a day to commemorate the working class struggle and is marked with marches and rallies worldwide.

In Los Angeles, taxi drivers have vowed to shut down LAX airport and trogueros (truck drivers) will be closing the harbor. Demonstrations are being planned in both major and smaller cities throughout the country, including Los Angeles, San Francisco, Dallas, Chicago and New York. Wherever possible, students and workers are planning both individual and group action. Many small businesses, particularly in the Mexican community, will be closing.

On the weekend of April 22, organizers will meet in Chicago to form a national network to continue this momentum. Following the meeting, there will be a press conference in Washington, D.C., on April 24, the date that Congress reconvenes.

In New York City, the Million Worker March Movement and the Troops Out Now Coalition, which were planning a May 1 rally and march from Union Square, voted to support the immigrant rights movement and the "Great American Boycott" action. The coalitions had held a march and rally last year to revive May Day and were actively making plans to march again this year. Chris Silvera, secretary treasurer of Teamsters Local 808 and president of the National Teamsters Black Caucus, proclaimed, "We support and embrace this movement." His union local is hosting the May 1 Great American Boycott 2006 Coalition, which is composed of the many immigrant communities of New York City including Latino, Filipino, South Asian, African, and Caribbean communities.

Nationally organizers are making plans to politically and legally support any worker or student who is retaliated against for their participation in activities [emphasis added].

PRO-IMMIGRATION SPIN

Over the years, the media have massaged the descriptive language in the reportage of immigration issues. The use of the terms "illegal alien" and "undocumented immigrant" and "undocumented worker" in published news accounts is a case in point. A search of major newspapers in Nexis conducted in early May 2008 revealed that "undocumented worker" or "undocumented immigrant" appeared in 2,749 hits within a recent 5-year span (2003-2008) in which the term was used at least 3 times in the cited source (in other words, the search terms appear in each published account a minimum of three times). The same 5-year period (2003-2008) turned up 835 hits of "illegal immigration" in major newspapers. The choice of "undocumented" worker or immigrant is a preferred descriptive term of major newspaper editors in referring to illegal aliens. A separate 5-year search of major newspapers from 1985-1990 revealed that "illegal alien" was used in 2,546 hits and "undocumented worker" or "undocumented immigrant" was cited in 558 hits in which each term appeared at least three times in the referenced source.

One Florida state official, Sen. Frederica Wilson, introduced a bill to prohibit the "official use of the term 'illegal alien.'"[9] Other Latino activist groups, such as the National Association of Hispanic Journalists (NAHJ), have likewise condemned the press for using "illegal alien" and described it as a pejorative term. According to the NAHJ:

> As protesters march in the streets and debate intensifies in Congress over how to fix the nation's immigration laws, the National Association of Hispanic Journalists calls on our nation's news media to use accurate terminology in its coverage of immigration and to stop dehumanizing undocumented immigrants.
>
> NAHJ is concerned with the increasing use of pejorative terms to describe the estimated 11 million undocumented people living in the United States. NAHJ is particularly troubled with the growing trend of the news media to use the word "illegals" as a noun, shorthand for "illegal aliens" [sic] Using the word in this way is grammatically incorrect and crosses the line by criminalizing the person, not the action they are purported to have committed. NAHJ calls on the media to never use "illegals" in headlines.
>
> Shortening the term in this way also stereotypes undocumented people who are in the United States as having committed a crime. Under current U.S. immigration law, being an undocu-

mented immigrant is not a crime, it is a civil violation. Furthermore, an estimated 40 percent of all undocumented people living in the U.S. are visa overstayers, meaning they did not illegally cross the U.S. border.

In addition, the association has always denounced the use of the degrading terms "alien" and "illegal alien" to describe undocumented immigrants because it casts them as adverse, strange beings, inhuman outsiders who come to the U.S. with questionable motivations. "Aliens" is a bureaucratic term that should be avoided unless used in a quote.

NAHJ, a 2,300-member organization of reporters, editors and other journalists, addresses the use of these words and phrases by the news media in its Resource Guide for Journalists.

Author William McGowan captured the gist of the media elite's coverage of immigration-related issues in his 2001 book, *Coloring the News: How Crusading for Diversity Has Corrupted American Journalism*. In his chapter on immigration, McGowan points out that:

> Many of those espousing multiculturalism, including many journalists, would like to think that the new diversity paradigm is an extension of the old Progressive social ideal, updated to reflect new social, political and cultural realities. Yet nothing could be further from the original Progressive vision than the romantic idealization of ethnic hyphenation. And liberal journalists of the past, who beat back the nativist contention that immigrants weren't capable of assimilating, would find it disorienting to hear their successors argue that assimilation is no longer necessary or even desirable, and that those holding this point of view are guilty of cultural intolerance or nostalgia.
>
> Were it less ideological, the journalistic establishment might acknowledge that public anxiety

about the heavy immigration isn't without some foundations. The demographic transformation such immigration has set in motion is unprecedented in America, turning a majority white nation with European cultural roots into a nonwhite plurality with no shared cultural heritage. No other country in history has ever willingly attempted, much less accomplished, a social makeover on this scale. According to polls, most Americans — including most Hispanics — feel uneasy about high rates of immigration and virtually open borders, believing that the harm resulting from such a situation outweighs the gains. Dismayed by the policy dilettantism of political elites, the majority of Americans also resent the fact that they have never been consulted about, much less allowed to debate, the merits of immigration policy with the vigor that the current situation warrants. As Nathan Glazer wrote in the *New Republic*, "When one considers present immigration policies, it seems we have insensibly reverted to mass immigration without ever having made a decision to do so."[10]

Examples of the pro-immigration coverage in leading newspapers, such as the *Washington Post* and *New York Times*, illustrate the negative spin on local anti-illegal immigrant initiatives. Pamela Constable's article on the front page of the Maryland edition of the *Washington Post*, May 6, 2008, headlines: "Immigrants Feel Less Welcome in Frederick." The first few paragraphs set the tone for the rest of the article:

> In just over a decade, Frederick County has been transformed from a bucolic, timeless community of dairy farms and strawberry festivals to a fast-paced mosaic of high-tech firms and housing developments, Pilates classes and exotic eateries, mega-stores and McDonald's.
>
> The changes have also brought thousands of Hispanics, some legal immigrants and others not,

who have migrated up Interstate 270 to meet the demand for construction and service jobs. Until now, the county has handled the influx with outreach classes in schools and community policing programs. Chic Hispanic restaurants flourish in downtown Frederick, and working-class Latinos have remained relatively invisible.

Suddenly, however, their presence is igniting a controversy that some fear could escalate into the kind of war over illegal immigration that has torn apart Prince William County. In the past month, the Frederick County sheriff has joined with federal authorities to identify and deport illegal immigrants, and county commissioners have proposed legislation to ban free translation of county business and require public schools to track down students who are in the United States illegally.[11]

Other articles and editorials appearing in the *Washington Post* have seized on the "fear" factor that immigrants now experience as a result of more aggressive enforcement of local, regional, and national immigration laws. One *Washington Post* headline read: "Fear Seizes Pr. William Immigrants — Legal and Not." Another more recent series of articles, "Careless Detention" by *Washington Post* staff writers Dana Priest and Amy Goldstein examine the extent to which "indigent laborers" (legal or illegal) are receiving poor medical treatment for severe health problems. One article's subhead captures the tone of the series: "As tighter immigration policies strain federal agencies, the detainees in their care often pay a heavy cost." The real question is whether or not American taxpayers should foot the bill for health coverage of illegal aliens, a point which seems lost on Priest and Goldstein. To paraphrase Cornell University labor economist Vernon Briggs, Jr., on this coverage, the emphasis news accounts place in covering immigration issues is based on what benefits and advances the interests of immigrants (illegal or legal) rather than considering is it good for the national interest?

NATIONAL ASSOCIATION OF
HISPANIC JOURNALISTS (NAHJ)

Founded in 1982, the National Association of Hispanic Journalists (NAHJ) organized to represent Hispanic journalists working for news organizations and to pressure media outlets to increase the numbers of Latino journalists. The background and mission of NAHJ is posted on the organization's website:

> NAHJ continues to pursue its mission with zeal, striving to bring more Hispanics into newsrooms across the country and to aid those already in the field, professionally and culturally. Advocating for the fair treatment of Hispanics and of journalists, the board regularly interacts with industry and national leaders.

> In October of 2002, NAHJ called on the news industry to increase dramatically the employment of Latino journalists during the next five years by announcing the creation of the Parity Project. Through the Parity Project, NAHJ identifies cities where Latinos are underrepresented in the newsrooms but make up a significant portion of the population, and works jointly with existing print and broadcast outlets, area journalism schools, foundations and Latino community leaders to develop comprehensive model programs that will increase Latino newsroom presence and influence. NAHJ's first partner on the project was the E.W. Scripps Company.

> [NAHJ] is dedicated to the recognition and professional advancement of Hispanics in the news industry. Established in April 1984, NAHJ created a national voice and unified vision for all Hispanic journalists.

> NAHJ is governed by an 18-member board of directors that consists of executive officers and regional directors who represent geographic areas of the United States and the Caribbean. The

national office is located in the National Press Building in Washington, D.C.

NAHJ has approximately 2,300 members, including working journalists, journalism students, other media-related professionals and journalism educators.

The goals of the association are:

◅ To organize and provide mutual support for Hispanics involved in the gathering or dissemination of news.

◅ To encourage and support the study and practice of journalism and communications by Hispanics.

◅ To foster and promote a fair treatment of Hispanics by the media.

◅ To further the employment and career development of Hispanics in the media.

◅ To foster a greater understanding of Hispanic media professionals' special cultural identity, interests, and concerns.

NAHJ is constantly adding to its list of exciting programs. They include:

◅ Regional workshops and seminars

◅ National Convention and Career Expo

◅ Mid-career and professional development programs

◅ Online job bank

◅ Journalism awards

◅ Internship and fellowship listings

◅ Student journalism workshops

◅ Newsletter

◅ Scholarships[12]

NATIONAL ASSOCIATION OF MULTI-ETHNIC DIVERSITY (NAMIC)

One trade organization that has worked to empower "people of color" in the telecommunications industry is the National Association of Multi-ethnic Diversity (NAMIC). The

NAMIC website describes the purpose and background of the trade association:

> Empowering Today's Multi-ethnic Diversity in Communications... NAMIC works to ensure that our industry reflects our world.
>
> The National Association for Multi-Ethnicity in Communications — NAMIC is a 501(c)(6) trade association that was founded in 1980. NAMIC educates, advocates and empowers for multi-ethnic diversity in the telecommunications industry through its 17 nationwide chapters. NAMIC welcomes existing and aspiring broadband and new media professionals to our membership roster. Members are cable operators, programmers, hardware suppliers, telecommunication and new media professionals and entrepreneurs. Our members come from customer contact offices, executive suites and every position in-between. They are of every race, multiple cultures — and they are all committed to a future in which these differences are strengths.
>
> NAMIC focuses locally to create change globally.
>
> Chapters across the United States are NAMIC's foundation. Membership is comprised of more than 1,500 professionals in 17 chapters throughout the country. NAMIC chapters cover the following areas: Atlanta, Chicago, Denver, Dallas, Detroit, Mid-Atlantic, New England, New York, Central Pennsylvania, Minnesota, Miami, Philadelphia, San Antonio, San Francisco Bay Area, Southern California, St. Louis and Western Pennsylvania. In addition to local chapter affiliation, all members belong to the national organization. Multiple chapter memberships are available for an additional fee.
>
> NAMIC is continually growing and working toward change.

NAMIC's success lies in not only focusing on industry-wide initiatives, but also in our commitment to individuals. Our leadership development programs give the tools for professional growth directly to employees, ensuring people of color will be a major part of the power base in the new millennium. After taking the pulse on issues of interest locally, NAMIC chapters work to build skills, create networking opportunities, participate in innovative programs and cultivate and develop leaders. NAMIC chapters provide important connections to local communities and keep members informed and in touch.

UNITY

The 2008 conference of UNITY, the largest gathering of journalists of color, was promoted as "a new journalism for a changing world."

The UNITY '08 Convention, July 23-27, 2008, will be the largest gathering of journalists of color. Nearly 10,000 journalists and media executives will meet to discuss timely issues affecting journalism and the media industry.

UNITY: Journalists of Color, Inc. is a coalition of the four alliances, the Asian American Journalists Association, the National Association of Black Journalists, the National Association of Hispanic Journalists and the Native American Journalists Association. Our mission is to advocate fair and accurate news coverage about people of color, and aggressively challenge the industry to staff its organizations at all levels to reflect the nation's diversity.

The UNITY '08 Convention includes booths and exhibits by national media organizations and major corporations (ABC, CNN/*Time*, Cox Enterprises, Chrysler, Coca Cola, Eli Lilly, NBC Universal, NPR, Philip L. Graham Fund, General Motors, and Novo Nordisk).

According to the UNITY website, UNITY '08 workshops offer the following for attendees:

◄ Changing Faces: Representing Minorities in the Media

Citizen Media: Entrepreneurial Ventures Plug Gaps in Local News

◄ Coalition or Demolition? The Impact of Immigration on Black-Latino Relations

◄ Cultural Competency: Turning Theory into Action

◄ Does the Color of Your Skin Matter: The Challenge of Race in the Locker Room

◄ All the gays are white, all the people of color are straight, but some of us are brave: Lesbian, Gay Bisexual and Transgender People of Color

◄ Presumption of Guilt: The Treatment and Coverage of Muslims in America

◄ The Changing Face in Editorial Cartoons

◄ The Journalist as Activist: Is Independence Still Valued

◄ These Kids Today: Covering Teens, Young Adults, and the Whole Podcast Generation

◄ What's so dark about Africa, anyway?

Other UNITY 2008 workshops are offered by corporate sponsors with panel discussion over breakfast or lunch:

◄ Activism and Blogging Panel Breakfast, *sponsored by General Motors*

◄ The Buying Power of People of Color Panel Breakfast, *sponsored by The Coca-Cola Company*

◄ How to Get a Media Grant, *sponsored by The Ford Foundation*

◄ The Diabetes Explosion: A Call to Action for Journalists of Color, *sponsored by Novo Nordisk*

◄ Lunch workshop, *sponsored by ABC, Inc.*

NATIONAL ASSOCIATION OF MINORITY MEDIA EXECUTIVES (NAMME)

The National Association of Minority Media Executives (NAMME's) focus is to host an annual conference and other programs to advance the interests of ethnic minority executives in the mass media. The NAMME website promotes annual conferences and goals under the theme "Transforming Leaders... Transforming the Industry":

> Each year, NAMME's Annual Conference combines executive development with discussions of cutting-edge industry issues. The conference also provides participants with an opportunity to meet and network with other managers and executives of color.
>
> NAMME is an influential organization of media managers and executives of color working in newspapers, broadcasting, magazines and online media. We are a multicultural group with members of all races. Our 400 members range from middle managers to newspaper publishers and broadcast general managers, as well as media entrepreneurs. More than 90 percent of its membership is African-American, Hispanic, Asian American and Native American, with African Americans and Hispanics being the two largest groups.
>
> As managers and executives of color in media we share a common commitment:
> ◄   To increase the number of people of color in the management ranks
> ◄   To craft innovative solutions to industry challenges
> ◄   To equip ourselves and the next generation of leaders with the skills and knowledge to master complex jobs and advance professionally, and
> ◄   To transform the industry to be more inclusive, accurate and fair in the coverage of communities of color.
>
> Yet today, our voices of leadership remain far too uncommon, our faces far too few. This conference will shed light on important issues rarely considered through the prism of diversity and

offer insights and perspectives critical to the success of media organizations going forward.

MAYNARD INSTITUTE FOR JOURNALISM EDUCATION

Named after Robert C. Maynard, the former editor of the *Oakland Tribune*, the Maynard Institute offers training programs for journalists "in recognition of the need to increase the number of managers of color in the news industry." The following corporations, foundations, and news organizations have served as generous sponsors of the Robert C. Maynard Institute for Journalism Education:

> Akonadi Foundation; *Arkansas Democrat-Gazette*; Belo Corporation, Community Newspaper Holdings, Inc.; Cox Newspapers, Inc.; The Ford Foundation; Gannett Co., Inc.; Philip L. Graham Fund; John S. and James L. Knight Foundation; Knight Ridder, Hearst Newspapers; Landmark Publishing Group; Lee Enterprises, Inc.; The McClatchy Company; McCormick Tribune Foundation; Media General; Media News Group, Inc.; North Jersey Media Group; Tribune Company; Morris Publishing Group; The New York Times Company; Samuel I. Newhouse Foundation; Pulitzer, Inc.; Scripps Howard Newspapers; *Times Herald-Record*; Times Mirror Foundation; and the *Washington Post*.

CONCLUSION

The mass media serves as a critical link in the open-borders, mass immigration network. The well-established liberal orientation of the media elite and the egalitarian leanings of the news culture well serve the interests of ethnic-immigrant activists and others in the open-borders network. As professional adversaries against authority, journalists are by their very nature sympathetic to the plight of the "oppressed" — Third World indigents, refugees, asylum seekers, and migrants fleeing (legally or illegally) repressive regimes in an attempt to start over in the "land of milk and honey." The ethnic balkanization of journalists within national news organizations, given the proliferation of ethnic journalist trade associations, co-serves the ethnic minority interests in the journalism profession and greater communities of "color" at the expense of the national interest.

Endnotes

1. Tim Groseclose and Jeffrey Milyo, "A Measure of Media Bias," *Quarterly Journal of Economics* (November 2005): 1191.
2. http://www.mediaresearch.org/biasbasics/biasbasics3.asp
3. David H. Weaver and G. Cleveland Wilhoit, *The American Journalist: A Portrait of U.S. News People and Their Work* (Bloomington, IN: Indiana University Press, 1986): 26.
4. S. Robert Lichter, Stanley Rothman, and Linda S. Lichter, *The Media Elite: America's New Powerbrokers* (Bethesda, MD: Adler and Adler, 1986)
5. Aaron Wildavsky, *The Rise of Radical Egalitarianism* (Washington, D.C.: American University Press, 1991): 116.
6. http://en.wikipedia.org/wiki/The_Bell_Curve
7. Wildavsky, 1991: 117.
8. http://en.wikipedia.org/wiki/Great_American_Boycott
9. "Phrase 'Illegal Alien' Faces Exile," *Tampa Tribune*, March 1, 2007: 10.
10. William McGowan, *Coloring the News: How Crusading for Diversity Has Corrupted American Journalism* (San Francisco, CA: Encounter Books, 2001): 182, 211.
11. http://www.washingtonpost.com/wp-dyn/content/article/2008/05/05/AR2008050502405.html
12. http://www.nahj.org/aboutnahj/ourhistory.shtml

7

THE SOUTHERN POVERTY LAW CENTER

∽๛๛

Life without prejudice, were it ever to be tried, would soon reveal itself to be a life without principle. For prejudices... are often built-in principles.

—**Richard Weaver**

O NE IDEOLOGICALLY DRIVEN NONPROFIT organization that skillfully overshadows other far-left groups on the "educational" nonprofit landscape is the Southern Poverty Law Center (SPLC). Founded, directed, and staffed by left-wing zealots, the SPLC serves a unique role in the open-borders network. It aggressively promotes a multicultural, multiracial agenda in every political, cultural, and social sphere of America's national fabric. The SPLC thrives off its adversaries, raising millions of dollars annually to combat the nebulous twin categories of "hate groups" and "intolerance," which form the operational core of the SPLC's programs and public activities.

To the unsuspecting individual, the SPLC seems non-partisan and ideologically neutral. The reality is that the SPLC, founded by radical egalitarians, primarily core "activists" in the civil rights movement, actively bolsters the fanatical dogma of political correctness, the activities of which mirror the Ministry of Truth in Orwell's *1984*. Reflecting the radical orientation of its staff, the SPLC vigilantly strives for broad "social change" of American society. Its ultimate goal is the transformation of the United States from a majority European-based culture to a multiracial Third World colony.

The following chapter explores the ideological agenda of the SPLC. It highlights the SPLC's persistent campaign to discredit the immigration-restriction movement, reveals some of the SPLC's questionable fundraising practices, and dissects the falsehood of the SPLC as an objective, non-ideological institution.

THE FORMATIVE YEARS

The SPLC, according to Wikipedia.org, "was founded in 1971 by Morris Dees, Joseph J. Levin Jr., and civil rights leader Julian Bond as a civil rights law firm."[1] The SPLC carved out a unique political niche as the nation's leading monitor of and aggressive litigant against far-right "extremists" and "white supremacist" organizations in the U.S. Over the span of 37 years, the SPLC has eclipsed other hard-left organizations that monitor far-right fringe groups in the U.S. As a self-identified "watchdog" organization, championing the intertwined causes of "civil rights" and "human rights," the SPLC actively undermines *any* effort that poses a challenge to radical egalitarianism. Mainstream immigration reform activists are one of several SPLC targets. The SPLC routinely labels citizen-activists, such as the Minutemen — reformers who seek reductions in legal immigration levels and vigorous enforcement of current immigration laws (blocking, arresting, detaining, and deporting illegal aliens) — as intolerant "extremists," "bigots," and "white supremacists."

Dees built his reputation in the fundraising profession by working as a chief fundraiser for the McGovern campaign in 1972 and as national finance chairman for Sen. Ted Kennedy's presidential bid in the 1980 Democratic primary. His success in direct mail fundraising is largely the result of cultivating an important left-wing constituency, namely wealthy, civil rights activists and other stalwart egalitarians.

Some of Dees's former associates are among his staunchest critics. According to Mike Hudson of the *Roanoke Times*:

To his critics, Dees is not so much a crusader for justice as a slick showman who uses fears of racial violence to enrich himself and his organization. They say SPLC is primarily a fund-raising machine that sucks donations away from other civil rights organizations. SPLC, these detractors say, does little to address difficult issues — such as voting rights and affirmative action — that are of more concern among poor and minority Americans than the acts of scattered Ku Klux Klan groups and right-wing militias.

Stephen Bright of the Southern Center of Human Rights, an Atlanta-based anti-death-penalty group, calls Dees "a fraud and a con man" who has "milked a lot of very wonderful, well-intentioned people."

A scathing article in the November 2000 *Harper's Magazine* quoted one critic who called Dees the "Jim and Tammy Faye Bakker of the civil rights movement." The article charged that SPLC relies on emotional pleas that suggest the organization is under terrible financial stress, skirting the fact that SPLC is the wealthiest civil rights group in America.[2]

Today, with a multi-million dollar budget, a large staff, and modern fortress-fortified six-story office building headquartered in Montgomery, Alabama, the SPLC has grown from a small legal office combating local segregation into a massive national operation tracking various movements on the political right. Today, its adversarial targets span a broader range of activists on the right than from its narrow inception of thwarting the white-robed members of the Invisible Empire. The SPLC's scope extends across a broad spectrum of grassroots Middle America. As an organization that at one time exclusively monitored Klan and neo-Nazi factions under the banner of "Klanwatch," the SPLC has evolved to conquer a wider scope of adversaries, namely anyone who is considered "intolerant" of left-wing causes. This vast category includes (but in no way is limited to) anti-abortion activists, cultural conservatives, pro-family advocates, immigration reform activists, religious conservatives, and assorted political gadflies on the right.

Underscoring their surveillance and monitoring activities, the SPLC vigorously promotes a society without borders, in essence, a nation with an undefined nationality and unlimited diversity; a nation which no longer distinguishes alien from citizen. The SPLC's website features its quarterly *Intelligence Report* on "hate groups" — what it characterizes as the "racialist, patriotic, and anti-Semitic" fringe of the far-right — and tracks various "hate crimes" from coast to coast. A "hate crime" by SPLC standards could be any ethnic slur that was uttered during a bar fight, or a college prank that some intoxicated undergraduates committed during a frat party, or the latest "noose" displaying incident. In seeking to criminalize "hate speech" and shore up valuable connections with local, state, and federal agencies, the SPLC regularly conducts seminars and workshops on the "terrorist threat" of domestic "hate groups." It briefs law enforcement agencies on a regular basis.

The SPLC's spin-off project, Tolerance.org, has cemented itself in the education establishment and provides supplemental materials to educators for classroom instruction. Tolerance.org offers a range of advice in combating "hate" and "intolerance." For example, the website notes that "[h]istorical and modern day images often contain hidden messages about us, about others, and about our world. These subtle lessons lie just beneath the surface. In order to see them, we must replace passive consumption of images with critical analysis. We can no longer accept a sculpture or a logo at face value. We must dig deeper. We must ask questions about why we perceive things the way we do." In the "Images in Action" section of "Planet Tolerance," the Tolerance.org website asks visitors, "When is a Saturday afternoon game demeaning?" Next to the question is a logo of the Washington Redskins, an NFL franchise.[3]

BILL AYERS, THE WEATHER UNDERGROUND, AND THE SPLC

To get a sense of the ideological agenda that defines

much of the SPLC's activities, the "Teaching Tolerance" website includes a revealing interview with 1960s militant William Ayers. As a former leader of the Weather Underground, Ayers was one of several fugitives from justice after the militant organization began a series of bombings that targeted the U.S. government in the early 1970s. In a brief biographical description, the interview merely refers to Ayers as an "education activist." The beginning of the interview, however, notes, "At age 20, Bill Ayers literally walked out of jail into his first teaching position. Throughout his career as a civil rights organizer, radical anti-Vietnam War activist, teacher and author, Ayers has developed a rich vision of teaching that interweaves passion, responsibility and self-reflection."[4] One infers from this account that, as a bomb-wielding militant, Ayers has been passionate in his militancy, responsible for turning himself in to authorities after more than a decade on the run as a fugitive from justice, and self-reflective in reminiscing about his unrepentant Weather Underground activities.

Ayers' militant past as a member of a domestic terrorist organization, one that was actively bombing government and military structures 30 years ago, is a legacy that he fondly recollects in his autobiography *Fugitive Days: A Memoir*, published in the fall of 2001 right around the terrorist events of 9/11. Ronald Radosh explains:

> Poor Bill Ayers. His timing could not have been worse. Just when his widely publicized memoir of his days as a terrorist was coming out, our nation suffered its worst terrorist assault ever. Indeed, the very morning of the attack, the *New York Times* printed a fawning profile of Ayers and his comrade in terror, Bernardine Dohrn. Under the headline "No Regrets for a Love of Explosives," accompanied by a large color photo of the couple, Ayers boasts that he bombed New York City's police headquarters in 1970, the Capitol building in 1971, and the Pentagon in 1972 — and proudly adds, "I don't regret setting bombs. I feel we didn't do enough." Asked whether he would

do it again, he answers, "I don't want to discount the possibility." Or, as he puts it in *Fugitive Days: A Memoir,* "I can't imagine entirely dismissing the possibility."[5]

Ayers describes the purpose of the Weather Underground in a posting on his blog: "[t]he catalytic radical student group of its day, the Weather Underground rose, hot and angry, to — in our own terms — smite the war-mongers and strike against the race-haters." In the years since his terrorist activities against the U.S. government, Ayers, like many '60s radicals, has reinvented himself as a "distinguished educator" and now holds a respected position as professor of education at the University of Illinois at Chicago.

During the Teaching Tolerance interview, Ayers' response to the following question underscores the relevance that ex-'60s militants place on "educational reform" for "social justice."

> *Q: How effective is the education system as a vehicle for bringing about social change?*
>
> **A:** Because I began teaching right after my release from jail, I've always linked teaching to social justice. There's a whole group of teachers who came out of the '60s who asked themselves, "What can I do with my life that would be consistent within an agenda of social change and hopefulness towards a more humane social order?" The most common choice has been to teach; teaching is seen as an extension of their involvement in social change.
>
> Unfortunately, despite that idealism and hopefulness, you end up with institutions that are not geared towards *liberation* or a vision of teaching as I've described it but are geared towards re-producing the social *injustices* and *inequities* that exist. For a lot of radical teachers, that's where the conflict and pain and burnout come in.
>
> It's important to remember the lessons of organizing for racial justice — and that the struggle is often hard. A lot of teachers my age have dis-

covered that, even though it feels hopeless at times, kids know who cares and parents know who cares. In the end, that becomes its own reward—you struggle against the injustices and you also provide hope and opportunity [emphasis added].[6]

In her autobiography, *Flying Close to the Sun*, Cathy Wilkerson, another former Weather Underground fugitive, describes the sordid ordeal of March 6, 1970, the day in which her parents' Greenwich Village townhouse collapsed into dust and rubble after a pipe bomb filled with dynamite, nails, and a blasting cap accidentally ignited, killing fellow Weather Underground militants Diana Oughton, Ted Gold, and Terry Robbins.

Wilkerson reflects on the atmosphere of a three-day conference in Cleveland during the summer of 1969. She found Ayers inspiring as a speaker but "could not...follow the next step in his reasoning" [quoting Ayers],

> We're not urging anybody to bring guns to Chicago, we're not urging anybody to shoot from a crowd, but we're also going to make it clear that when a pig gets iced that's a good thing, and that everybody who considers himself a revolutionary should be armed, should own a gun, should have a gun in his home.[7]

Daniel Flynn, in *A Conservative History of the American Left*, attributes the following quote to Ayers: "Kill all the rich people.... Bring the revolution home, kill your parents, that's where it's really at."[8]

As this author pointed out in a posting on VDARE (see below), Democratic presidential candidate Barack Obama tried to deflect his ties to Ayers, which surfaced during a debate with Sen. Hillary Clinton.

> During the recent debate in Philadelphia between Barack Obama and Hillary Clinton, Obama downplayed the fact that he had affiliations with 60s radical Bill Ayers, a former leader of the Weather Underground. Obama dismissed a question about

his connections to the ex-fugitive by describing Ayers as "a guy who lives in my neighborhood." Questions about Obama's association with Ayers had surfaced in recent months on various blogs.

Obama not only served alongside Ayers as a director of the Woods Fund, a Chicago-based anti-poverty organization, but according to the *Chicago Sun-Times*, "In the mid-1990s, Ayers and Dohrn hosted a meet-and-greet at their house to introduce Obama to their neighbors during his first run for the Illinois Senate. In 2001, Ayers contributed $200 to Obama's campaign."

Although the latest media coverage of Ayers contains a critical edge, much of this reportage puts the past in a nostalgic context and emphasizes how Ayers and his wife Bernadine Dohrn, also a former Weather Underground fugitive, have transformed themselves into establishment figures and are now "distinguished professors" at the University of Illinois [at] Chicago and Northwestern University.

Dohrn once praised the Charles Manson massacres of 1969 in which actress Sharon Tate and others were brutally butchered to death. During a 1969 speech to the "War Council" in Flint, Michigan, Dohrn made her controversial remarks regarding the Manson Family murders: "Dig it. First they killed those pigs, then they ate dinner in the same room with them. They even shoved a fork into the victim's stomach! Wild!"

The 2003 Academy Award-nominated documentary *The Weather Underground*, a candid retrospective of former Weather Underground leaders reminiscing about their militant past, begins with Dorhn speaking before a press conference in the early 1970s: "Hello, I'm going to read a declaration of a state of war...within the next 14 days we will attack a symbol or institution of American injustice."

The headline in [the] *Washington Post*: "Former 60s Radical Is Now Considered Mainstream in Chicago" confirms that ex-60s fugitives, contrary to F. Scott Fitzgerald's proclamation that there are "no second acts in American life," often re-establish themselves as distinguished and productive members of American society. As long as the cause is fighting "social injustice," "racism," and "inequality," then the spin on some ex-fugitive's militant past will be excused as one bad acid trip or some other youthful indiscretion. Imagine the *New York Times* or *Washington Post* describing some anti-government militants on the Far Right in comparable terms.[9]

Navigate around the Teaching Tolerance site and without difficulty one recognizes the politically correct dogma that dominates the nature of the posted selections: *"Making Numbers Count: How social justice math can help students transform people, politics and communities;" "Does My Town Have a Racist Past? How students can convert the shameful history of sundown towns in America into a rich opportunity for setting the record straight;" "Caroline is a Boy: From kindergarten to college, transgender and gender-nonconforming students face many challenges in school and classroom settings;" "Discovering Lewis and Clark: As the nation celebrates the bicentennial of the Lewis and Clark Expedition, educators across the country should be asking what one Oregon teacher does: 'Is this a celebration for Native Americans?'; and "Drawing on Justice: The Comic Book Project encourages students to address social issues in their lives and schools with art and creativity."*

One featured selection from the Spring 2008 issue of *Teaching Tolerance*, "Making Numbers Count," directs the reader to another site: radicalmath.org. The website states the purpose of radicalmath.org:

RadicalMath.org was launched in April 2006 by Jonathan Osler who at the time was teaching at a public high school in Brooklyn, NY. Since then this website has had over 1 million page views.

Radical Math Teachers are educators who work to integrate issues of economic and social justice into our math classes, and we seek to inspire and support other educators to do the same.

We believe that math literacy is a civil right, and that our nation's failure to provide students, especially low-income youth of color, with a high-quality math education, is a terrible injustice.

We are committed to making sure our classrooms are places that are nurturing for all students, that celebrate different cultures, histories, and styles of learning, and that reflect the just societies we are hoping to bring about through our own lives and teaching practices.

We encourage our students to ask the question: "What are the problems that my community is facing, and how can I use math to understand and help solve them?"

We seek to foster a love of mathematics in our students and to ensure they become mathematically literate. We also prepare our students for math-based college majors and careers.

We believe that it is possible to teach math from a social justice perspective and at the same time cover state and national standards, prepare students for standardized tests (which we don't necessarily support), and allow for the exploration of mathematical ideas on abstract, theoretical, experimental and artistic levels.

On the radicalmath.org site, the following is one of several examples of "problems" which students are provided in order to introduce the three "R's" (Revealing Racist Roots):

Revealing Racist Roots: The Three R's for Teaching about the Jena 6 — This mini-unit was developed by Joyce Sia and Rico Gutstein, teachers at the Greater Lawndale/Little Village School for

Social Justice in Chicago, and is part of a teaching guide on the Jena 6 put out by the Network of Teacher Activist Group (including NYCORE — the New York Collective of Radical Educators). The central problem of the unit is to *find the probability of selecting an all-white jury in Jena.*

Public opinion polls continue to show that illegal immigration has become a major public issue in recent years. Immigration reform efforts in Congress, as has been noted, have run into intense opposition from the vast range of organized groups pushing for unlimited "diversity" and unrestricted immigration levels. Hence, the latest targets of the SPLC's surveillance operations are America's leading immigration reformers. Leaders in the immigration reform movement are repeatedly linked to political extremists and fringe political subcultures (such as skinheads and militant malcontents), however removed from reality the relationship may be on flimsy allegations, rumors, and innuendos in an attempt to discredit the motives of these reformers and therefore undermine the legitimacy of reducing U.S. immigration levels.

In addition to aggressive litigation battles that the SPLC wages in court against its opponents, as a Non-Governmental Organization (NGO), the SPLC is highly successful in charitable fundraising. The success it has enjoyed in fundraising as a nonprofit organization is largely due to catering to wealthy left-wing donors and cultivating a base of supporters for its activities. The range of activities includes monitoring domestic operations (the activities of their adversaries), promoting multicultural education materials via the SPLC's "Teaching Tolerance" project website, and disrupting the work and lives of their political adversaries.

(To set the record straight, the SPLC's aggressive work to pursue their political adversaries impacted my own career in January 2005. My employment as a newspaper editor and part-time researcher [with my former employer, a major news organization] was severed as a result of the SPLC's smear campaign in direct contact with a former employer. The disclosure of working for a third publication, one the SPLC tagged as a "white supremacist" journal, prompted an immediate termination by my primary employer after nearly 3 years of dedicated employment and subsequently after some 15 years of full and part-time employment with another employer. I decided to accept a forced resignation from Eagle Publishing given a few minutes notice to either submit my resignation [thus receiving the value of limited stock benefits] or face an immediate firing and forego any severance benefits. When asked what were the grounds of the termination, the response from Eagle's Vice President of Operations was, "we think you know why." In a free society, individuals should have the right to freely express their views without repercussions, such as loss of employment, rank, or status. An employer's right to hire and fire should not trump an employee's right to free expression. One should not fall prey to the sociological pressures of conformity in the workplace simply because one's perspectives are considered politically incorrect.)[10]

SELECTIVELY TARGETING
"EXTREMISTS"

How many editors or journalists on the political left in recent memory have lost jobs or had to abandon career prospects for being too radical or too far-Left? How many Left-wing scholars have lost employment as a result of the SPLC's activities, labeling radical leftists as "extremists" and leveraging their employers with sustained pressure to fire such an individual? Dr. Kevin MacDonald, a professor of psychology at California State University at Long Beach, is a frequent target of the SPLC and the subject of extensive coverage in the SPLC's *Intelligence Report*. In a search of the SPLC site, MacDonald's name surfaces nine times. Ward Churchill, the discredited "political activist" and anarchist, was professor of ethnic studies at the University of Colorado at Boulder from 1990-2007 when UC found Churchill guilty of "research misconduct." The SPLC's website has no mention of Churchill's "research misconduct."

One technique the SPLC has used to monitor the activities of their adversaries is to attend conferences and meetings of their political foes often using aliases for the purpose of gathering and spreading gossip, innuendo, and rumor on their arch-enemies. Much of this activity, planting news articles and cultivating journalistic sources, is primarily for the calculated intent of generating revenue to further "combat hate, intolerance, and discrimination through education and litigation." The SPLC has fostered a refined image in the mass media as an objective source of reliable information on the fringe of America's far-right political movements. Scholars and writers who question the empirical validity of universal human equality (recognizing that inequality is a natural condition among human groups) are targets of the SPLC's wrath. Critics across the ideological spectrum have identified an ideologically driven agenda in the SPLC's modus operandi. As in the case of immigration reformers, the SPLC traffics in manufactured or distorted information by alleging "links" between them and fringe "hate" groups on the far-right for the purposes of smearing and discrediting their adversaries.

The SPLC has been highly active in attacking its opponents in the public arena. It has included in its vast survey of "hate groups" the Michigan State University chapter of Young Americans for Freedom, pro-life Roman Catholics, and evangelical religious conservative groups. Whereas Sen. Joseph McCarthy's critics successfully spawned a political backlash over "guilt by association" attacks, the SPLC has waged effective smear campaigns against their adversaries with specious "guilt by linkage" affiliations with minimal repercussions. It has crafted a crusading reputation for its legal victories against far-right "extremist" groups, often winning hefty judgments in the process, and it has skillfully used these cases, which in many instances are uncollectible judgments, as the basis of its bountiful fundraising efforts. The SPLC is considered to be the largest endowed civil rights group in the U.S.

AN "F" GRADE IN PHILANTHROPIC PRACTICES

Wealthy leftists serve as the financial lifeline among the SPLC's major donors. Annually, the SPLC receives charitable grants from numerous left-wing endowments and raises substantial returns from direct-mail solicitations. According to financial reports available from guidestar.org, the SPLC listed over $45 million in total revenue collected in 2006 and has amassed financial assets totaling $192 million.[11] The SPLC's professional fundraising fees are nine times greater than its legal fees. In 2006, it spent nearly $2.5 million on "postage and shipping," which is more than the total compensation for officers and directors ($1.7 million).[12] Also in 2006, the SPLC spent over $900,000 in telemarketing and mailing list fees.

As a nonprofit (501c3) organization, the SPLC has come under scrutiny for its fundraising and charitable practices. Over the years "charity watch" groups have given the SPLC low ratings for stashing away charitable funds. It routinely receives low marks from Charity Navigator in its "efficiency rating." The American Institute of Philanthropy has given the SPLC an "F" for "continuing to raise money while sitting on large reserves."[13]

According to the Better Business Bureau website, the SPLC has refused to participate in the BBB's charity review: "Despite written Better Business Bureau requests in the past year, this organization either has not provided current information or has declined to be evaluated in relation to the BBB's charity standards. While participation in the BBB's charity review efforts is voluntary, the BBB believes that this lack of cooperation may demonstrate a lack of commitment to transparency. Without the requested information, the BBB cannot verify if the charity adheres to the BBB charity standards."[14]

In the high-profile case of Joan Little, a black woman who was on trial for the 1974 murder of a white prison guard, according to *Facts on File World Digest*, the SPLC "was reported April 18 to have raised $200,000 in defense funds for Little. A Southern Christian Leadership Conference (SCLC) spokesman said that this fund-raising effort was a 'rip-off' because $20,000 would have been sufficient for the trial. (The total was reported May 5 to be up to $300,000.) The SCLC further contended, it was reported April 18, that the Law Center had reneged on a promise to give it 30 percent of the funds raised and that it had withdrawn its active support of Little."[15]

In November 2006, the Capital Research Center (CRC) issued a report by Matthew Vadum on the SPLC, scrutinizing its philanthropic sources. The CRC noted:

> By nonprofit standards, SPLC has an enormous endowment of more than $152 million, according to its 2005 annual report. Its IRS Form 990 for the fiscal year ended Oct. 31, 2005, shows that the center took in gross receipts of $49.8 million that year, $29.7 million of which consisted of contributions and grants. According to its balance sheet, by Oct. 31, 2005, its total assets had ballooned from $173.2 million at the beginning of the fiscal year, to $189.4 million by year's end. SPLC's endowment is so large that it reported endowment income of nearly $3.5 million, including interest income of $728,356. Although SPLC bills itself as a civil rights law firm, it devotes only a fraction of its resources to actual legal work. Of the $28.9 million in expenses it declared for the year ended Oct. 31, 2005, only $4.5 million went to "providing legal services for victims of civil rights injustice and hate crimes," and $837,907 for "specific assistance to individuals" in the form of "litigation services," according to its Form 990. Roughly half of its expenditures, $14.7 million, were devoted to "educating the general public, public officials, teachers, students and law enforcement agencies and officers with respect to issues of hate and intolerance and promoting tolerance of differences through the schools." In the same period, SPLC paid attorney Morris Dees $297,559 in salary and pension-plan contributions. On the list of nonprofit "employees who earned more than their organization's chief executive," (part of the *Chronicle of Philanthropy*'s annual survey of top nonprofit executive salaries, published September 28), Dees ranked 48th in the nation.

Funders of [the] SPLC include Cisco Systems

Foundation (at least $1.6 million since 2001), Picower Foundation (at least $1.7 million since 2000), the Richard and Rhoda Goldman Fund ($535,000 since 2001), and the Grove Foundation ($450,000 since 2001).[16]

SCATTERSHOT TARGETS

The SPLC has targeted a wide spectrum of individuals and groups in recent years, from mainstream conservative activists to media personalities. The list includes CNN anchor and show host Lou Dobbs; the American Enterprise Institute; Dinesh D'Souza, a prize-winning syndicated columnist; Dr. J. Philippe Rushton, professor of psychology at the University of Western Ontario and a Guggenheim Fellow; Dr. Kevin MacDonald, a professor of psychology at California State University at Long Beach; a publisher of traditional Roman Catholic literature; attorneys; a former magazine publisher; fundamentalist evangelical Christians; and conservative activist Howard Phillips.

Arguably the SPLC has focused more recent attention on CNN anchor Lou Dobbs and the leaders of the immigration reform movement, Rep. Tom Tancredo (R-CO); John Tanton,[17] the founder of the Federation for American Immigration Reform (FAIR); former Democratic governor of Colorado Richard Lamm; Minutemen founders Jim Gilchrist and Chris Simcox; FAIR's Executive Director Dan Stein; NumbersUSA; and the American Immigration Control Foundation. Tanton, the publisher of *The Social Contract*, served as editor for its first 8 years. Lamm and Tanton, longtime conservationists, have been active in liberal environmental causes.

David Horowitz's discoverthenetworks.org website aptly describes the SPLC's political agenda as catering to left-wing interests:

> In the SPLC's view, American society remains irredeemably rife with bigotry aimed at racial and ethnic minorities.... More recently, however, it is the SPLC that has found itself on the defensive. Critics from across the political spectrum charge

the Center with betraying its professed commitment to advancing civil rights. The SPLC levels accusations of racism unjustly, branding as "bigoted" many groups and individuals whose only crime lies in their refusal to embrace the SPLC's leftwing agenda. Some accuse the SPLC of pursuing revenue rather than justice, by orchestrating fundraising campaigns that exaggerate the prevalence of racism to ensure a steady stream of donations from the Center's alarmed supporters. The SPLC consistently claims to detect evidence of white racism infesting virtually every crevice of American society. The Center states, for instance, "Like most of the southeastern U.S., Georgia has seen an explosion in Hispanic immigration in recent years — over a half million since 1990 alone. As hate groups exploit the racial tension stemming from the area's growth, locals have launched violent attacks against immigrant workers." The SPLC's ideological biases are evident in its map of Active U.S. Hate Groups. Although the SPLC denounces extremist religious groups like the Jewish Defense League and Westboro Baptist Church, no mention is made of even a single extremist Muslim group. Similarly, while far-right groups like the Council of Conservative Citizens are tagged as hate groups, the SPLC withholds judgment on extremist leftwing groups. The aforementioned Intelligence Project, an SPLC initiative that monitors hate and extremist groups around the United States, is conspicuously selective in its scrutiny. Whereas rightwing groups are routinely the subjects of Intelligence Project reports, the political left, as evidenced by the dearth of critical literature, is above suspicion. In 2003, for instance, the SPLC hosted a forum called "Right-Wing Extremism in a Transatlantic Perspective," which, as one SPLC report noted, sought to

develop strategies to combat "the radical right."
Of the radical left, no mention was made.

As part of its transparently one-sided approach to outing alleged hate groups, the SPLC is not above flinging fictional charges against its ideological adversaries. One particularly egregious example was a 2003 article called "Into the Mainstream," featured in the SPLC's quarterly magazine, *Intelligence Report*. Authored by fringe leftist Chip Berlet, this tendentious report deliberately mangled quotes and omitted context, to make the case that "right-wing foundations and think tanks support efforts to make bigoted and discredited ideas respectable." Among the groups that came in for the SPLC's scorn was the Center for the Study of Popular Culture, and its founder, David Horowitz. After wresting, out of context, several of his quotes on the subjects of African Americans and slavery, the report charged Horowitz with a "selective rewriting of history" — a distortion so patently dishonest that it prompted Horowitz to pen an open letter to SPLC co-founder Morris Dees, wherein he answered the attack and called on Dees to apologize and remove the report from the SPLC's Web site. Dees complied on neither count. In support of the charge that the SPLC unfairly targets groups that do not share its politics, critics point to the Center's charitable treatment of leftwing groups. Radical organizations like United for Peace and Justice, for instance, are hailed as "social justice groups," a designation that also extends to feminist groups like Equality Now, a number of gay rights groups, Human Rights First, Amnesty International, and Jesse Jackson's National Rainbow/PUSH Coalition.[18]

SMEARING IMMIGRATION-REFORM ACTIVISTS

One SPLC newsletter from its "Intelligence Project" is *Immigration Watch*. Launched in September 2005, *Immigration*

Watch tracks "the explosive growth of the anti-immigration movement in the United States...providing current information about the rising extremism and anti-immigrant sentiment." Growing public concerns over illegal immigration has created a political vacuum for opponents of immigration reform efforts. Grassroots activists who seek reductions of annual immigration levels are scrutinized by *Immigration Watch* in terms of "exposing" a hidden "extremist" agenda on the part of leading immigration-restriction groups. Immigration reform activists are often described as promoting "hate" or identified as an affiliate of some "hate group." Peter Brimelow, a former editor at *National Review*, former editor at *Forbes*, and founder and host of the VDARE website, has also been identified as a "hate group." Lou Dobbs has been criticized for his nonstop coverage of illegal immigration. Pat Buchanan has likewise been criticized by Mark Potok, the director of the SPLC's "Intelligence Project." Potok and the *Intelligence Report* have tried to link the former co-host of CNN's "Crossfire" and regular MSNBC commentator to fringe "extremists" on the racialist right.

✧✧✧

Although the SPLC continues to bolster its image in the media and among government officials and law enforcement agencies as an impartial watchdog monitoring the activities of America's Far-Right activist fringe, the reality—documented in this chapter—is quite different.

As has been demonstrated with the SPLC's recent efforts to "monitor" the activities of immigration reformers, the quest to label as "racist" and "hate" any discussion of population or demographic trends as well as critiques of multiculturalism and current problems with U.S. immigration policies is an effective tactic of the radical Left to thwart any measure that would place annual limits on immigration. The SPLC maintains an aggressive ideological agenda to transform the culture and traditions of American society—from a legal heritage that seeks a balance between the rights of individuals and the interests of society, as grounded in Constitutionally protected rights of free speech, free expression and free association, to a futuristic society that represents the Marxian, totalitarian influence on America's political, legal and civic institutions in the quest to eradicate any group-based distinctions.

In his posthumously published book, *Life Without Prejudice and Other Essays*, Richard Weaver accurately observed that cultural *pluralism* and *autonomy* accentuate the significance of cultural freedom in free societies:

> For the freedom of cultures as wholes, two rights must be respected: the right of cultural pluralism where different cultures have developed, and the right of cultural autonomy in the development of a single culture. In a word, cultural freedom on this plane starts with the acknowledgement of the right of a culture to be itself. This is a principle deduced from the nature of culture, not from the nature of the state. Culture grows from roots more enduring than those of the political state.... Culture emerges out of climatic, geographical, ecological, racial, religious, and linguistic soils; a state may have to deal with them at the level where they enter into cultural expression.... In brief, cultural freedom as an integral part of the free society requires that distinctive cultures be allowed to preserve their homogeneity; that creators of cultural works should not be hobbled by political and sociological dogmas; and that in a given culture a tradition should be left free to find its own way of renewing itself. Violation of any of these shows a fundamental ignorance of what culture is and how it ministers to the life of the spirit.[19]

The Southern Poverty Law Center and its acolytes ultimately seek a society free of both cultural *pluralism* and cultural *autonomy*; one that is rooted in cultural Marxism and one that fundamentally enforces cultural uniformity — a borderless nation without a nationality committed to eliminating cultural and ethnic distinctions and expunging its European-based cultural heritage.

Endnotes

1. en.wikipedia.org/wiki/Southern_Poverty_Law_Center
2. Mike Hudson, "Nurturing Justice or Cashing In?," *The Roanoke Times*, August 27, 2003: A1.
3. www.tolerance.org/teach/?source=redirect&url=teaching tolerance
4. www.tolerance.org/teach/magazine/features. jsp?p=0&is=15
5. Ronald Radosh, "Don't Need a Weatherman; The Clouded Mind of Bill Ayers," *Weekly Standard*, October 8, 2001: 37.
6. www.tolerance.org/teach/magazine/features. jsp?p=0&is=15
7. Cathy Wilkerson, *Flying Close to the Sun: My Life and Times as a Weatherman*, (New York: Seven Stories Press, 2007): 292.
8. Daniel J. Flynn, *A Conservative History of the American Left*, (New York: Crown Forum, 2008): 305.
9. http://blog.vdare.com/archives/2008/04/18/from-urban-guerrillas-to-upstanding-establishment-citizens-bill-ayers-and-the-weather-underground-in-perspective/print/
10. www.vdare.com/misc/050922_lamb_events.htm
11. www.guidestar.org/FinDocuments/2006/630/598/2006-630598743-03a2755f-9.pdf
12. Ibid.
13. Thomas S. Brown, "Check Charities List Twice," *News-Journal*, December 9, 2006: 1B.
14. http://centralalabama.bbb.org/WWWRoot/Report. aspx?site=43&bbb=0463&firm=4222
15. "JoAnn Little on Trial for Murder," *Facts on File World News Digest*, May 24, 1975.
16. www.capitalresearch.org/pubs/pubs.html?id=581
17. For a detailed reply to the SPLC's criticisms of Dr. Tanton, see the Social Contract Press website: http://thesocialcontract.com/puppeteer.html"
18. www.discoverthenetworks.org/groupProfile. asp?grpid=6989
19. Richard Weaver, *Life Without Prejudice and other essays*, (Chicago, IL: Henry Regnery Company, 1965): 19, 37.

CONCLUSION

༄༅

A preponderating influence of foreigners is a sure
solvent of the existence of States. It takes away
from a people its most precious possession—its
soul.

—Gustave Le Bon

The crisis of the West is of a collapsing culture
and vanishing peoples, as a Third World that
grows by 100 million people—the equivalent of
a new Mexico—every eighteen months mounts
the greatest invasion in the history of the world.
If we do not shake off our paralysis, the West
comes to an end.

—Pat Buchanan

AMERICANS ARE LIVING IN AN AGE of unprecedented change.
Advances in modern technology have boosted their standard of living drastically over the past twenty years. Modern
conveniences of the personal computer, cellular phones,
Internet, GPS navigational devices, and other microelectronic
devices have enhanced our communications and comforts
and eased our interactions and mobility. To some extent, these
effortless luxuries compound our complacency as the challenges that await future generations are endlessly postponed.

The dilemma Americans face in the foreseeable future, however, is the unparalleled cultural, racial, and ethnic transformation of uncontrolled mass immigration. As the nation moves beyond the assimilation stage of the "Melting Pot" into the balkanized, crowded caldron of unassimilated ethnic competition, the future of America's founding population looks bleak. CIA Director Michael Hayden's speech at Kansas State University — which the *Washington Post* characterized as "new security challenges for the United States" as a result of the "civil unrest" of "swelling populations" and a "global tide of immigration" — included the following candid observations:

> Today, there are 6.7 billion people sharing the planet. By mid-century, the best estimates point to a world population of more than 9 billion. That's a 40 to 45 percent increase — striking enough — but most of that growth is almost certain to occur in countries *least able to sustain it,* and that will create a situation that will likely fuel *instability* and *extremism* — not just in those areas, but beyond them as well.

> There are many poor, fragile states where governance is actually difficult today, where populations will grow rapidly: Afghanistan, Liberia, Niger, the Democratic Republic of the Congo. That group — the population is expected to triple by mid-century. The number of people in Ethiopia, Nigeria, and Yemen is likely to more than double. Furthermore — just beyond the raw numbers — all those countries will therefore have, as a result of this, a large concentration of young people. *If their basic freedoms and basic needs — food, housing, education, employment — are not met, they could be easily attracted to violence, civil unrest, and extremism.*

> And through the fact of global migration, this impact of rapid population growth in Africa or Southeast Asia and elsewhere is not going to be confined to those places. It will be felt in the developed world as well. *Millions of young people*

134

from fast-growing, poorly developed countries will emigrate – legally and illegally – in search of economic opportunity, security, or political freedom.[1]

Our future will either resemble the national character of European-American traditions, firmly established by the founding settlers and their descendants, or mirror the Third World turmoil of multiethnic stratification comparable to contemporary Brazil. The march toward multiethnic stratification (unrestricted immigration from the Third World) is well underway.

Outraged American citizens, adversely impacted by the growing menace of illegal aliens in their communities, such as the residents of Hazelton, Pennsylvania; Prince William County, Virginia; and now Frederick, Maryland; are increasingly voicing their opposition to the open-borders lobby. This post-9/11 period of uninterrupted mass immigration to the United States prompted legislative action in the 109th and 110th Congress and a response from the Bush Administration. The highly organized mass-immigration, open-borders network—a coalition of religious, social, business, labor, legal, government, ethnic-immigrant, and radical activist groups— effectively blocked any attempt to secure the U.S. southern border in the absence of another blanket amnesty for untold millions of illegal aliens.

The growing presence of organized ethnic-immigrant interest groups will prove problematic for any long-range resolution of America's immigration crisis. As long as the federal government provides grants to groups like the National Council of La Raza, an open-borders, ethnic advocacy organization, any attempt to vigorously strengthen U.S. immigration laws and limit the influx of immigrants will ultimately fail. As *Human Events* noted last year:

> To most of the mainstream media, most members of Congress, and even many of their own members, the National Council of La Raza is no more than a Hispanic Rotary Club.
>
> But the National Council of La Raza succeeded in raking in over $15.2 million in federal

grants last year alone, of which $7.9 million was in U.S. Department of Education grants for Charter Schools, and undisclosed amounts were for get-out-the-vote efforts supporting La Raza political positions.

The Council of La Raza succeeded in having itself added to congressional hearings by Republican House and Senate leaders. And an anonymous senator even gave the Council of La Raza an extra $4 million in earmarked taxpayer money, supposedly for "housing reform," while La Raza continues to lobby the Senate for virtual open borders and amnesty for illegal aliens.

Congressman Ruben Hinojosa (D-TX) has introduced legislation, "The Hope Fund Act of 2007," which would provide $5,000,000 for La Raza in fiscal year 2008 and $10,000,000 for each fiscal year thereafter. The federal government is subsidizing our national destruction as federal subsidies are underwriting organizations in the open-borders network. The federal government's support for ethnic-immigrant advocacy groups contributes to further stalemate in resolving America's immigration problems.

George F. Kennan summed up the matter this way:
Unfortunately it appears, as things stand today, to lie beyond the vigor, and the capacity for firm decisions, of the American political establishment to draw any rational limits to further immigration. This is partly because the U.S. government, while not loath to putting half a million armed troops into the Middle East to expel the armed Iraqis from Kuwait, confess itself unable to defend its own southwestern border from illegal immigration by large numbers of people armed with nothing more formidable than a strong desire to get across it. But behind this rather strange helplessness there lie, of course, domestic-political pressures or inhibitions that work in the same direction: notably, the thirst for cheap labor

among American employers and the tendency of recently immigrated people, now here in such numbers that they are not without political clout, to demand the ongoing admission of others like themselves…the inability of any society to resist immigration, the inability to find other solutions to the problem of employment at the lower, more physical, and menial levels of the economic process, is a serious weakness, and possibly even a fatal one, in any national society.[2]

The interests and agenda of the open-borders network, which William R. Hawkins astutely noted in his important work *Importing Revolution: Open Borders and the Radical Agenda*, is now firmly enmeshed into the fabric of America's political culture. Overcoming the future security concerns that potentially would undermine America as a stable, unified nation by mid-century, as Michael Hayden implied in his recent address to a Kansas audience, can only leave those in attendance wondering about the future of their heartland communities.

Well, Toto, it looks as if we're not in Kansas any more!

Endnotes

1. www.washingtonpost.com/wp-dyn/content/article/2008/04/30/AR2008043003258.html
2. George F. Kennan, *Around the Cragged Hill: A Personal and Political Philosophy* (New York: Norton, 1993): 154-155.

APPENDIX

Organizations Supporting Amnesty for Illegal Aliens

The following list of organizations supporting amnesty for illegal aliens is available from the website of the Federation for American Immigration Reform (FAIR): fairus.org.

EMPLOYER ORGANIZATIONS

Agricultural Coalition for Immigration Reform (ACIR—employers)
"AICR urges your support of [AgJobs]...To meet the existing shortage of legal workers, and avoid the immediate need for a large number of guest workers, workers who can prove that they are experienced agricultural workers can earn the opportunity to obtain legal status...."
The Agricultural Coalition for Immigration Reform, made up of farming groups, paid Washington lobbyists $180,000 last year to work on the [AgJobs amnesty] issue, public records show.
Sacramento Bee, Dec. 17, 2003

American Health Care Association (AHCA—business)
"Our laws, therefore, should allow willing workers to enter our country and fill jobs for which U.S. citizens cannot be found."
Charles H. Roadman II, President and CEO of AHCA, press release, Feb. 12, 2004.

American Hotel & Lodging Association (AHLA—business)
"[AHLA]...seeks to reform the U.S. immigration system. Its primary mission [EWIC's] is to allow employers facing shortages of semi-skilled and unskilled ('essential worker') labor to hire workers from abroad."

American Nursery & Landscape Association (ANLA—business)
"The second and equally critical provision in [the AgJobs bill] is the 'earned status adjustment' program. This program is a logical and constructive approach to the reality of a largely undocumented workforce."

Essential Worker Immigration Coalition (EWIC—employers)
"EWIC (co-chaired by IFA Vice President, Government Relations John Gay) has two main goals: to reform the immigration system

139

to allow employers to bring in foreign workers when no American workers can be found and to create a mechanism for many of the millions of undocumented workers in our industries to be able to earn legal status."

International Franchise Association (IFA — business)
"[B]usinesses have found that employees they thought were authorized to work were in fact undocumented. This has caused significant disruptions for some employers as they have lost key employees or entire shifts of workers due to a government audit or raid." (see EWIC)

National Association of Manufacturers (NAM — business)
"The United States should not place artificial quotas or restrictions on employers' ability to hire or move people as needed."
Immigration Issue Brief, Jan. 2004

National Council of Chain Restaurants (NCCR — business)
"This is a positive development for the industry. I hear all the time from my members that the biggest problem they face is not being able to find enough workers, and this would certainly be a help."
— NCCR Director of Government Relations Scott Vinson, responding to President Bush's support for a limited amnesty for Mexicans living and working in the U.S., in *Nation's Restaurant News*, August 13, 2001.

National Council of Farmer Cooperatives (NCFC — employers)
Created by ANLA to work for AgJobs.

National Restaurant Association (NRA — business)
"As the nation's largest private-sector employer and largest employer of immigrants, currently 1.4 million, we believe that our nation's immigration policy should not only secure our borders, but also match willing employers with willing employees." Lee Culpepper, senior vice president of Government Affairs and Public Policy, Press Release October 23, 2002

Society of American Florists (SAF — employers)
"As a member of the Society of American Florists, I strongly support [AgJobs amnesty] because it will provide a stable and legal workforce, increase border security, and treat workers fairly.
"This legislation (AgJobs amnesty) really needs to pass this year."
Lin Schmale, SAF senior director of Government Relations in Greenhouse Product News.

U.S. Chamber of Commerce (business)
"We need a system of 'earned targeted adjustment' for undocumented workers that fill vital roles in our economy, which

would enable them to achieve legal status. We also need to expand permanent and temporary visas for workers to enter the United States legally to meet future workforce requirements." Randel Johnson, Chamber vice president for labor, immigration and employee benefits. Jan 7, 2004

LABOR ORGANIZATIONS

American Federation of Labor-Congress of Industrial Organizations (AFL-CIO—labor)
"The [SOLVE Act amnesty] bill includes reforms we in the union movement believe are absolutely necessary to address what is now an unworkable system." AFL-CIO President John Sweeney, press conference May 4, 2004.

American Federation of State, County and Municipal Employees (AFSCME—labor)
"RESOLVED: That there be legalization of the undocumented workers who are working hard, paying taxes and contributing to their communities and the nation." Resolution No: 98, 35th Int. Convention, June 2002.

Farm Labor Organizing Committee (FLOC—Latino labor)
"We have successfully campaigned for Toledo to make the Mexican *matricula consular*, an official ID for the city."

Hotel Employees and Restaurant Employees International Union (HERE—labor)
"UNITE and HERE have collaborated most recently in the Immigrant Workers Freedom Ride…" Press release, February 26, 2004. See UNITE. HERE and UNITE to merge in July 2004 to form UNITE HERE.

Laborers' International Union of North America (LIUNA—labor)
"The Laborers' International Union of North America applauds the comprehensive immigration reform bill…", Statement of Terence M. O'Sullivan General President LIUNA on the [SOLVE Act amnesty bill]. May 5, 2004

Service Employees International Union (SEIU—labor)
"SEIU was a driving force behind the AFL-CIO's decision to support legalization for hard-working, tax-paying immigrants. SEIU represents more immigrant workers than any other union, and has been a leading voice for immigration reform that rewards work and improves conditions for all working people."

Union of Needletrades, Industrial and Textile Employees (UNITE!—labor)

See HERE. HERE and UNITE to merge in July 2004 to form UNITE HERE.

United Farm Workers (UFW—labor)
"United Farm Workers President Arturo Rodriguez will join other national leaders of labor, ethnic and immigrant rights groups in... urging President Bush and Republican leaders in Congress to match their rhetoric favoring Latino immigrants with action on two popular bipartisan immigration reform bills: AgJobs and the DREAM Act." Press Release July 16, 2004

United Food and Commercial Workers (UFCW—labor)
"The position of the UFCW is simple and direct: we don't care about green cards, we care about union cards. We care about union contracts that guarantee dignity at work and a decent standard of living at home---regardless of race, gender, nationality or immigration status." International Secretary-Treasurer Joe Hansen, June 10, 2000

Ethnic Organizations

American Jewish Committee (AJC—Jewish religious)
"The AJC has reaffirmed its support for the principle of earned legalization for immigrants who have been residing in the U.S. unlawfully for a substantial period of time." Press release, Dec. 8, 2003

Arab American Institute (AAI—Arab ethnic advocacy)
AAI President Dr. James Zogby

Asian Pacific American Labor Alliance (APALA—Asian ethnic advocacy)
"Hard work should be rewarded. Immigrants, like other hard working American families, should have fair and equal access to opportunities, and be allowed to go as far as their talents will take them." Comment by APALA executive director, Gloria T. Caoile, on "Freedom Ride" for amnesty.

Asian Pacific American Legal Center (APALC—Asian legal assistance)

Catholic Legal Immigration Network, Inc. (CLINIC—religious, legal aid)

Central American Resource Center (CARECEN—Salvadoran ethnic, Los Angeles)
"[CARECEN]...educates the federal state and local public officials in addition to the community in general about the immigration

needs of the Central American refugee community. The program also advocates for fair humanitarian immigration laws."

Comite de Apoyo a los Trabajadores Agricolas (CATA — migrant farmworkers — Latino ethnic)
(CATA) is the non-profit arm of the Unión de los Trabajadores Agrícolas y de Hongo (UTAH).

Farmworker Justice Fund (Latino, civil liberties)

Hispanic Alliance for Progress (HAP — Latino ethnic)

The Latino Coalition (Latino ethnic)
"[The Bush immigration proposal] is a comprehensive and effective approach to address our immigration crisis," said TLC President Robert Deposada....The President's proposal offers workers already in this country without proper documentation the ability to legalize their status." Press Release, Jan. 7, 2004.

Leadership Education for Asian Pacifics (LEAP)

League of United Latin American Citizens (LULAC — Latino ethnic)
"LULAC supports the regularization of undocumented workers in the United States by periodically updating the Date of Registry, the reinstatement of Section 245(i) to allow immigrants to remain with their families while their applications are processed, along with the restoration of Food Stamps for legal immigrants." Adopted by the LULAC National Assembly on June 21, 2003.

Mexican American Legal Defense and Education Fund (MALDEF — Latino ethnic)
"MALDEF has continually advocated for an 'earned legalization.' Immigrants who demonstrate that they pay taxes, have a job, and pass a security test should be able to qualify for legal status." Katherine Culliton, legislative staff attorney, press release May 4, 2004.

National Asian Pacific American Legal Consortium (NAPALC — Asian ethnic)
"We look forward to working with members of Congress from both parties and the Administration to enact the SOLVE Act [amnesty] into law." Karen Narasaki, Pres. NAPALC, press release, May 4, 2004.

National Association of Latino Elected & Appointed Officials (NALEO — Latino advocacy)

National Council of La Raza (NCLR — Latino ethnic)
"...NCLR feels that this bill [(SOLVE) Act of 2004] offers the

best approach to immigration reform, providing a balanced and moderate approach to immigration reform. It...makes legality the norm by bringing hardworking immigrants out of the shadows and allowing them to earn their legal status, and by creating the necessary legal channels for needed workers to enter the U.S. in the future." Raul Yzaguirre, NCLR President and CEO, press release May 4, 2004.

National Federation of Filipino American Associations (NFFAA — Filipino ethnic)

National Korean American Service & Educational Consortium (NKASEC — Korean ethnic)

Organization of Chinese Americans (OCA — Chinese ethnic) "In February, OCA passed a resolution in support of comprehensive immigration reform that included significantly reducing the backlog of family-based immigration, creating a path for legalization of undocumented immigrants, and creating additional programs for individuals to enter legally into the United States to work temporarily or permanently." Press Release, May 20, 2004.

RELIGIOUS ORGANIZATIONS

American Friends Service Committee (AFSC — Quaker religious) "[AFSC's] Project Voice combines local and national organizing, education, and outreach campaigns to achieve a strategic impact on key immigration and refugee issues, including legalization...."

Lutheran Immigration and Refugee Service (LIRS — Lutheran religious) "We look forward to working with Congress and the White House to craft an immigration system that unites families, ensures worker rights and human rights, allows immigrant workers to live freely and openly in our society, and gives those willing to contribute to our economy and society a true path toward citizenship in the United States." Statement by LIRS President Ralston H. Deffenbaugh Jr. on the SOLVE amnesty bill, press release May 4, 2004.

National Interfaith Committee for Worker Justice (NICWJ) "The struggle for acceptance and justice endured by past immigrants continues today with some 8.5 million immigrants deprived of the right to apply for citizenship. Often separated from their families and victimized by unscrupulous employers, America's newest class of immigrants is suffering." Kim Bobo,

NICWJ executive director, press release August 27, 2003.

U.S. Conference of Catholic Bishops (USCCB—Catholic religious)
"We urge our federal policymakers to revise our nation's immigration laws and policies in a manner which includes the following elements: legalization for the maximum number of persons in an undocumented or irregular legal status;… enforcement policies;…revision of the 1996 immigration laws;… repeal of mandatory detention of immigrants;…and a religious worker visa program which is permanently authorized…" (Resolution, November 16, 2000)

CIVIL LIBERTIES AND OTHER ORGANIZATIONS

American Immigration Lawyers Association (AILA—immigrant advocacy)
"Why we need [SOLVE Act amnesty]: Legalizing undocumented workers is good for America." Posted on AILA InfoNet at Doc. No. 04050467 (May 4, 2004)."

Center for Migration, Ethnicity and Citizenship at New School University

Coalition for Humane Immigrant Rights of Los Angeles (CHIRLA)
"CHIRLA works with day laborers to create safe and organized environments for seeking work.… Its goal is to gain a broad legalization program for the six million undocumented workers and their families residing in USA."

Illinois Coalition for Immigrant and Refugee Rights (ICIRR— immigrant services)
"Legalization will unleash the economic potential of Illinois' immigrant communities." ICIRR Executive Director, Joshua Hoyt, Crains Chicago Business, May 10, 2004

Leadership Conference on Civil Rights (LCCR)

Migration Policy Institute/NYU Law School Muzaffar Chishti, Director

National Employment Law Project (NELP—labor, civil liberties)
"NELP's newly-expanded guide provides step- by-step directions for drafting state and local day labor legislation… [Agenda] should include legalization for workers currently present in the U.S., wage and labor protections for new and established workers, family reunification provisions, as well as a path to citizenship for immigrants here and those to be admitted."

National Immigration Forum (NIF—open borders)
"Immigration reform would address a range of workforce

realities — legalizing a workforce that is here to stay anyway, providing more legal visas for workers to come in the future, and providing for the temporary employment of foreign workers who help American employers in sectors of the economy that provide seasonal jobs."

National Immigration Law Center (NILC — defense of illegal aliens)
"NILC facilitates the development of a shared national policy agenda and strengthens the advocacy presence of immigrant rights organizations at the federal level."

National Network on Immigrant and Refugee Rights (NNIRR — refugees, civil liberties)
"We need a comprehensive program that allows undocumented immigrants from all nationalities and living in the U.S. to obtain legal permanent residency."

Services, Immigrant Rights Network, and Education (SIREN)
San Jose, CA, immigrant rights activists.

Source: Federation for American Immigration Reform
www.fairus.org/site/PageServer?pagename=iic_
immigrationissuecentersa5ad?&printer_friendly=1

ACKNOWLEDGMENTS

The author owes a special debt of gratitude to my family, close friends, and associates for their encouragement. I am especially indebted to Ted O'Keefe, who drafted two chapters for this project. His thoroughness as an experienced copy editor is unsurpassed. It has been a rewarding experience to work with him on various projects over the years. To my colleagues on the *Social Contract*, especially our editor Wayne Lutton, thanks for giving me the breathing space to work on this important project. I offer my appreciation to the publisher and the American Research Foundation for the opportunity to undertake this worthy venture. I would like to thank Louis T. March for reaching out and initiating this project and marshalling it to completion. Finally, thanks to Peter Brimelow, Peter Gemma, and Roger Pearson for their inspiration, insights, and camaraderie over the years. The late Sam Francis, friend and former colleague, is deeply missed. His unfortunate death spawned an unforeseen calamity of events that Sam could and would have prevented from unfolding. Losing Sam has proven to be a colossal setback for our collegial endeavors.

ABOUT THE AUTHOR

Kevin Lamb, a graduate of Indiana University with degrees in journalism and political science, is the managing editor of *The Social Contract*. He served as managing editor of *Human Events* (2002-2005) and as a library assistant for *Newsweek* (1989-2002). An extern of the National Journalism Center (1988), he served in the United States Marine Corps Reserves from 1981-1986 and received an honorable discharge at the rank of sergeant.

His writings have appeared in the *Asian Wall Street Journal*, *National Review*, *Chronicles*, *Society*, *Human Events*, *Mankind Quarterly*, *Middle American News*, *Conservative Review*, *The Journal of Social, Political and Economic Studies*, VDARE.com, *The Social Contract*, and *Right Now!*

He assisted Sam Francis in assembling and marshalling to press a seminal collection of essays, *Race and the American Prospect: Essays on the Racial Realities of Our Nation and Our Time*, published in 2006.

An avid reader, aficionado of classical orchestral music, and editor in exile, he is presently working on several long-range writing projects. As the founding editor of *The Occidental Quarterly*, he resigned as editor in September 2007 in the wake of a purge of the editorial staff.